SELECTED POETRY OF

QATEEL SHAFAI

With original Urdu text, Roman and Hindi transliteration and poetical translation into English

IN THE SAME SERIES:

★ **Selections from SHAKEEL BADAUNI**

★ **Selected poems of SAHIR LUDHIANVI**

★ **Selected poems of ALLAMA IQBAL**

★ **Selected poems of FAIZ AHMAD 'FAIZ'**

★ **Selected poetry of QATEEL SHAFAI**

★ **Selected poetry of BAHADUR SHAH 'ZAFAR'**

ALSO IN URDU:

★ **TARKASH** (Poetry) **by Javed Akhtar**

★ **NADI KE PAAR** (Poetry Urdu + Hindi) **by Salman Akhtar**

STAR PUBLICATIONS PVT. LTD.

New Delhi.110002

SELECTED POETRY OF

QATEEL SHAFAI

With original Urdu text, Roman and Hindi transliteration and poetical translation into English

قتیل شفائی کی شاعری

क़तील शफ़ाई
की शायरी

English translation by :

Khwaja Tariq Mahmood

Compiled by :

Amar Varma

Selected Poetry of
QATEEL SHAFAI
(Multilingual edition)
English translation by Khwaja Tariq Mahmood
Star, New Delhi, 2020

ISBN : 81-7650-080-1

Published by:
STAR PUBLICATIONS PVT. LTD.
4/5 Asaf Ali Road, New Delhi, 110002

This Edition : 2020
Price: Rs. 350.00 (in India)
£ 14.95 (in U. K.)

Sole distributors in the U.K.:
INDIAN BOOK SHELF
55 Warren St., LONDON W1T 5NW
(Phone: 020 - 7380 0622, e-mail : indbooks@aol.com)

Photo typeset by Wasi Prints, New Delhi.

QATEEL SHAFAI

(1919 : 2003)

Urdu poetry is today most popular, not only among Urdu knowing people, but also among these millions of people who love poetry in any language and form. Songs from Indian films have created interest in Urdu poetry all over the world, and names of poets like Ghalib, Sahir Ludhianvi, Shakeel Budauni, Faiz Ahmad Faiz, Allama Iqbal etc. etc. are well known in every home.

Qateel Shafai is another name in the category of these poets, whose poetry has been presented in many forms, in books, in dance recitations, in albums, and above all in Indian and Pakistani films.

Qateel Shafai was born in Haripura Hazara (now in Pakistan) in 1919, and presented his poetry in more than 15 collections. He had started his life as a small shopkeeper in Rawalpindi (Pakistan), but had been taking part in literary activites ever since. He was honoured with a number of literary awards. In 1947, he was invited by a film producer to write songs for his films, and since then he wrote songs for many films.

This collection of his selected poems is our humble tribute to this great poet of the year.

—Publishers

قتیلؔ شفائی

مُطرب، نغمہ گر، شگفتہ طبع، شیریں گفتار قتیلؔ شفائی ترقّی پسند شعراء کے قافلے میں اہلِ قافلہ کے ہمسفر بھی ہیں اور اُن سے جُدا بھی۔ اگر جذباتی اور نظریاتی معاملات میں اِن کے دل و دماغ اپنے ہمرہوں کے ہم آہنگ ہیں تو اظہار اور ترسیل کے مقامات میں قتیلؔ کی آواز منفرد بھی ہے اور ممتاز بھی، اوّل تو کچھ یوں ہے کہ گویا قتیلؔ نے کسی پلیٹ فارم یا چھت پر کھڑے ہو کر اپنے پڑھنے سننے والوں کو وعظ و تلقین سے مستفید نہیں کیا بلکہ اُنہیں کے ساتھ فرش پر بیٹھ کر میٹھی کڑوی باتیں کی ہیں۔ پھر ان باتوں میں بھی غیظ و احتجاج کی کڑواہٹ کم ہے۔ درد محبّت کی مٹھاس زیادہ، دُوسرے یوں ہے کہ جو کچھ لکّھا ہے ''بلا شرکت غیرے'' لکّھا ہے، جو کچھ کہا ہے کسی کے کہنے پر نہیں اپنے دل کی شہادت پر کہا ہے۔ الفاظ کے طرفہ بیل بُوٹے نہیں بنائے، افکار میں کسی بال کی کھال اُتارنے کی کوشش نہیں کی، جنس اور لاشعور کے جوہڑ میں ڈبکیاں نہیں لگائیں۔ دھیمے سُر لگائے ہیں اس لیے نغمہ کبھی بے سُرا نہیں ہونے پایا، ہلکے رنگ استعمال کیے ہیں اس لیے تصوّر کا کوئی نقش آنکھ میں نہیں کھٹکتا، یہی سادگی اور کم نمائی اُن کے فن اور شخصیت کی نمایاں خوبی ہے۔ یہی شیرینی اور رسیلا پن اس کا زیور۔

سُنتے آئے ہیں کہ کسی شاعر یا ادیب کا صحیح مقام آنے والی نسلیں متعیّن کرتی ہیں، یہ بات اپنی جگہ مسلّم لیکن یہ دیکھنا بھی لازم ہے کہ سخنور نے اپنے زمان و مکان کے دائرے میں کتنے دلوں میں گھر کیا ہے اور اس کے کہے سے کتنے پڑھنے، سننے والوں کو محسوس ہوا کہ گویا یہ بھی میرے دل میں ہے، اس اعتبار سے قتیلؔ شفائی کا کلام اپنے وقت کی مخلوق میں یقیناً مقبول اور محبوب ہے۔ عاقبت کی خبر خدا جانے۔

فیض احمد فیضؔ

शायर के बारे में

"क़तील" शफ़ाई 24 दिसम्बर 1919 को स्थान हरीपुर हज़ारा में पैदा हुए। उनका ख़ानदानी नाम औरंगज़ेब ख़ाँ है। "क़तील" शफ़ाई का पालन–पोषण बड़े अच्छे घरेलू माहौल में हुआ। प्रारंभिक शिक्षा गर्वनमेंट हाई स्कूल हरीपुर हज़ारा (अब पाकिस्तान में) में हासिल की।

"क़तील" साहब ने "शफ़ाई" का शब्द अपने उस्ताद हकीम मौहम्मद "शफ़ा" के सम्बन्धों से अपने नाम का अंग बनाया। यद्यपि उन का हकीम "शफ़ा" साहब से इस्लाह शागिर्दी का ज़माना बहुत ही संक्षिप्त रहा परन्तु क़तील शिफ़ाई की पैत्रिक कर्तव्य–परायणता ने कभी इस बात को स्वीकार न किया कि वह "शफ़ा" से बेवफ़ाई करें।

"क़तील" शफ़ाई बचपन ही में अपने पिता के स्नेह से वंचित हो गए। इसी कारण उन्हें बड़ी मुसीबतों का सामना करना पड़ा। पिता के देहांत के बाद क़तील साहब ने पढ़ाई छोड़कर स्पोर्ट की दुकान खोल ली। बाद में बज़ाज़ी का काम शुरू किया और असफल होने में वतन छोड़कर रावलपिण्डी चले गए। वहाँ "मरी ट्रांसपोर्ट कम्पनी" में साठ रुपये मासिक वेतन पर नौकरी कर ली। 1946 में मासिक "अदबे–तलीफ़" के चौधरी नज़ीर अहमद ने "क़तील" को लाहौर बुला लिया और "अदबे–लतीफ़" का सह–सम्पादक नियुक्त किया।

"क़तील" की पहली ग़ज़ल लाहौर के साप्ताहिक "स्टार" में प्रकाशित हुई जिसके सम्पादक "क़मर" जलालाबादी थे। जनवरी 1947 में लाहौर के एक फ़िल्म निर्माता ने अपनी फ़िल्म के गाने लिखवाने के लिए क़तील को लाहौर बुला लिया और फिर वह वहीं के हो रहे। अब तक उनके कई कविता–संग्रह प्रकाशित हो चुके हैं। उनके एक संग्रह "मुतरिबा" पर पाकिस्तान का सबसे बड़ा साहित्यक पुरस्कार "आदम जी एवार्ड" भी मिला। उन्हों ने विभिन्न फ़िल्मों के सर्वोत्तम गीतों पर सोलह एवार्ड प्राप्त किए। फ़िल्मी शायरी के साथ–साथ फ़िल्म–निर्माण में भी "क़तील" साहब का निकटतम सम्बंध रहा।

इस दौर में जिन बहुत कम शायरों को भरपूर सफलता मिली है उनमें "क़तील" शफ़ाई का नाम प्रमुख है।

क़तील शफ़ाई का देहान्त 2003 के आरंभ में हुआ। और इस प्रकार उर्दू का एक और लोकप्रिय शायर हम सब से दूर चला गया।

–सम्पादक

INDEX فہرست

उन गेसुओं की छाँव.....
IN THE SHADOW............ 12-15 .... اُن گیسوؤں کی چھاؤں

हम को अपनी पुरफ़िशानी....
WHY, O WORLD............ 16-19 .... ہم کو اپنی پُرفشانی

अंधेरे छोड़कर.....
LEAVING DARKNESS.......... 20-23 .... اندھیرے چھوڑ کر میں

कभी न ख़त्म हुई.....
THOUGH OUR.................. 24-27 .... کبھی نہ ختم ہوئیں

शाम के साँवले चेहरे.....
WE MIGHT WELL............ 28-31 .... شام کے سانولے چہرے

यूँ लगे दोस्त.....
I REGARD YOUR ANGST........ 32-35 .... یوں لگے دوست

तरस रहा हूँ मैं.....
I LONG FOR MY LOVED........ 36-39 .... ترس رہا ہوں میں

लोगों में एहतियात.....
AMONG PEOPLE............ 40-43 .... لوگوں میں احتیاط

लिख दूँ जो सरापा.....
IF I WRITE ABOUT............ 44-47 .... لکھ دوں جو سراپا

तूफ़ां कोई उठे.....
LET NO ONE TAKE............ 48-51 .... طوفاں کوئی اُٹھے

ज़िंदगी की दलदल है.....
MAN IS WEEK AGAINST...... 52-55 .... زندگی کی دلدل ہے

शाम–ए–नज़्ज़ारा.....
FROM DUSK TO DAWN....... 56-59 .... شام نظارہ

क्या इश्क़ था.....
WHAT WAS THAT LOVE....... 60-63 .... کیا عشق تھا

मैंने पूछा.....
I HAD WONDERED............ 64-67 .... میں نے پوچھا

तुझे भी डर है किसी का.....
IF YOU ARE AFRAID........... 68-71 .... تجھے بھی ڈر ہے کسی کا

सदमा तो है मुझे.....
I AM ALSO SHOCKED......... 72-75 .... صدمہ تو ہے مجھے

मरहला रात का.....
WHEN NIGHT.................. 76-79 .... مرحلہ رات کا

मैं समंदर भी हूँ.....
I AM ALSO AN OCEAN......... 80-83 .... میں سمندر بھی ہوں

जो भी गुचा तिरे.....
EVERY SMILE............ 84-87 .... جو بھی غنچہ ترے

नहीं धड़का मुझे.....
I AM NOT AFRAID............ 88-91 .... نہیں دھڑکا مجھے

रास्ते याद नहीं राहनुमा.....
I SCARE REMEMBER........92-95 ....راستے یاد نہیں راہنما

कोई मक़ाम–ए–सकूं.....
ON OUR WAY.................96-99 ....کوئی مقامِ سکوں

इक–इक पत्थर जोड़ के.....
BRICK BY BRICK...............100-103...............اک اک پتھر جوڑ کے

वफ़ा के शीश महल.....
ON A HIGH PEDESTAL........104-107..................وفا کے شیش محل

यार क्यों गुरेज़ां है.....
TO TREAD THE RIGHTEOUS..108-111.............یار کیوں گُریزاں ہے

बज़ाहिर बज़्म–आराई.....
APPARENTLY ENCLAVES....112-115................بظاہر بزمِ آرائی

जब भी दरिया बारिशों के.....
WHENEVER..................116-119...........جب بھی دریا بارشوں کے

मेहरबानी से अगर पेश.....
EVEN IF SOME PEOPLE........120-123...............مہربانی سے اگر پیش

हर शय से बेगाना अच्छा.....
'TIS GOOD......................124-127..............ہر شے سے بیگانہ اچھا

दो चेहरगी.....
DOUBLE FACE................128-131.........................دو چہرگی

कर्ब–ए–अना.....
EGO'S PAIN....................128-131...........................کربِ انا

तहक़ीक़.....
RESEARCH......................132-135...........................تحقیق

दिलासा.....
CONSOLATION...................132-135...........................دلاسہ

तारकीन.....
EMIGRANTS.....................136-139...........................تارکین

कैरेक्टर.....
CHARACTER.....................136-139...........................کیریکٹر

ख़ैर अगर चाहते हो.....
IF YOU WANT SAFETY..........140-143.......................خیر اگر چاہتے ہو

रची है रतजगों.....
THOSE WHO SHOW...........144-147...............رَچی ہے رَت جگوں

दिल वालों की बात.....
PEOPLE OF HEART.............148-151.................دل والوں کی بات

बे वफ़ाओं में तो नाम.....
BELOVED'S NAME..............152-155..............بے وفاؤں میں تو نام

मेरी आंखों में...
BELOVED HAS NEVER.........156-159...............میری آنکھوں میں

खनखनाते हैं.....
THOUGH GOBLETS.............160-163.................کھنکھناتے ہیں

हुक्मराँ मुझको बहारों.....
LET ME BECOME KING........164-167...............حکمراں مجھ کو بہاروں

जब तक वो झूमता.....
NOT UNTIL THAT CLOUD......168-171..................جب تک وہ جھومتا

थोड़ा सा ग़म.....
I ALSO SUFFER..................172-175...................تھوڑا ساغم

बात छेड़.....
TALK OF BELOVE'S...........176-179...................بات چھیڑ

उनके बग़ैर जी.....
WITHOUT BELOVED...........180-183...................اُن کے بغیر جی

हालात के क़दमों पे.....
A DAUNTLESS PERSON.......184-187..............حالات کے قدموں پہ

हुई न राह में हाइल.....
WEARINESS OF MY FEET.......188-191...............ہوئی نہ راہ میں حائل

ज़िंदगी के ग़म लाखों.....
MILLION WOES OF LIFE........192-195...............زندگی کے غم لاکھوں

दूर तक छाए थे बादल.....
THE WERE CLOUDS............196-199...........دُور تک چھائے تھے بادل

जब से असीर–ए–ज़ुल्फ़.....
EVER SINCE....................200-203...............جب سے اسیر زلف

वो शख़्स कि मैं जिससे.....
A PERSON FOR WHOM..........204-209...........وہ شخص کہ میں جس سے

जब उसके पास मिरा.....
WHEN MY MESSAGE.........208-211...........جب اس کے پاس مرا

सोचा था अपने आप.....
WE THOUGHT...................212-215...................سوچا تھا اپنے آپ

तिरे गले में अगर.....
IF AROUND YOUR NECK........216-219...................ترے گلے میں اگر

लूटा जो हमसफ़र.....
THE FELLOW TRAVELLER....220-223................لُوٹا جو ہمسفر نے

शब–ए–विसाल कुछ ऐसा.....
ON THE SIGHT..................224-227...............شبِ وصال کچھ ایسا

तमाम शह्र के रस्ते.....
LET ALL THE STREETS...........228-231...................تمام شہر کے رستے

जो तेरे प्यार का सौदा.....
WHOEVER ARE WITH.........232-235...............جو تیرے پیار کا سودا

धूप है, रंग है...
IS IT SIGHT COLOUR.......236-239...............دھوپ ہے، رنگ ہے

जिएगा कौन.....
WHO WILL LIVE...............240-243...................جیئے گا کون

आ ग़म–ए–जानाँ.....
COME O WORLDLY...........244-247...................آغمِ جانان

बहुत दिनों से.....
'TIS LONG SINCE..................248-251...................بہت دنوں سے

* * *

اُن گیسوؤں کی چھاؤں....

اُن گیسوؤں کی چھاؤں میں دم لینا چاہیے
تپتی رُتوں میں لطفِ اِرم لینا چاہیے

پھیلا ہے اِتنا حسن، کہ اس کائنات میں
انساں کو بار بار جنم لینا چاہیے

میں ہوں خدا پرست مگر کہہ رہا ہے دل
اِک بوسۂ جبینِ صنم لینا چاہیے

دیتے ہیں پھَل بدی کا جہاں نفرتوں کے پیڑ
نام اس دیار کا ہمیں کم لینا چاہیے

چاہے وہ کوئی ہو، مرا فتویٰ ہے یہ قتیلؔ
ظالم سے انتقامِ ستم لینا چاہیے

* * *

IN THE SHADOW.....

In the shadow of these tresses, we may take rest
In the blazing season, to savour beloved's fest

So much beauty is extant in the universe
We may be born and reborn in the beauty's quest

I idealise divinity, but heart wishes ever more
To idolise diety, my respect to attest

Where saplings of animosity spawn fruit of enmity
That habitat we may shun ,and treat as a pest

Not to let off the hook, even brought to book
Every tyrant, O "Qateel", to avenge and protest

* * *

Un Gesuoṃ Kī Chām̐va....

una gesuoṃ kī chām̐va meṃ dama lenā cāhie
tapatī rutoṃ meṃ lutfa-e-irama lenā cāhie

phailā hai itanā husna, ki isa kāyanāta meṃ
insāṃ ko bāra-bāra janama lenā cāhie

maiṃ hūm̐ khudā parasta magara kaha rahā hai dila
ika bosā-e-jabīna-e-sanama lenā cāhie

dete haiṃ phala baḍī kā jahāṃ nafaratoṃ ke peḍa
nāma usa dayāra kā hameṃ kama lenā cāhie

cāahe vo koī ho, mirā fatavā hai yaha "qatīla"
zālima se intaqāma-e-sitama lenā cāhie

* * *

उन गेसुओं की छाँव.....

उन गेसुओं की छाँव में दम लेना चाहिए
तपती रुतों में लुत्फ़-ए-इरम[1] लेना चाहिए

फैला है इतना हुस्न, कि इस कायनात में
इन्सां को बार-बार जनम लेना चाहिए

मैं हूँ ख़ुदा परस्त मगर कह रहा है दिल
इक बोसा-ए-जबीन-ए-सनम[2] लेना चाहिए

देते हैं फल बदी का जहां नफ़रतों के पेड़
नाम उस दयार[3] का हमें कम लेना चाहिए

चाहे वो कोई हो, मिरा फ़तवा[4] है यह "क़तील"
ज़ालिम से इन्तक़ाम-ए-सितम[5] लेना चाहिए

* * *

1. जन्नत का मज़ा 2. सनम (महबूबा, बुत) के माथे का चुम्बन
3. शहर 4. निर्णय 5. अत्याचार का बदला

ہم کو اپنی پُر فشانی....

ہم کو اپنی پُرفشانی کا صلہ کیوں کر ملے!
چاند پر جاکر بھی اے دُنیا ہمیں پتھر ملے

صحنِ گلشن کا یہ عالم تھا کہ جب آندھی رُکی
ہر طرف بکھرے ہوئے کچھ تتلیوں کے پَر ملے

رہبروں کے دم سے اَب راہوں میں اتنی بھیڑ ہے
سوچتے ہیں اپنے گھر کا راستہ کیوں کر ملے

کس کو اَب سجدوں کی حسرت کس کو ذوق بَندگی
سَر کے دشمن تھے سبھی جتنے بھی سنگِ در ملے

اُن کے ہاتھوں میں قتیلؔ اک دن چھری دیکھو گے تم
وہ منافق جو گلے لگ کر تمہیں اکثر ملے!

* * *

WHY, O WORLD.....

Why, O world, we are not rewarded for our diligence
We had asked for the moon, but met with stony silence

In the garden state, when the storm did abate
Feathers of butterflies were, scattered all the distance

Thanks to trekkers' leaders, tracks are overflowing
We wonder how at all we find our home with sense

Who can wish to prostrate, aspire to supplicate
Our head was hit with stone, as our way recompense

The hypocrites who often had met you so warmly
One day you find them, O "Qateel", come for your comeuppence

* * *

Ham Ko Apnī Purfiśānī....

hama ko apanī puarafiśānī kā silā kyoṅkara mile
cām̐da para jākara bhī ai duniyā hameṃ patthara mile

sahne gulaśana kā yaha ālama thā ki jaba āṃdhī rukī
hara tarafa bikhare hue kucha titaliyoṃ ke para mile

rahabaroṃ ke dama se aba rāhoṃ meṃ itanī bhīḓa hai
socate haiṃ apane ghara kā rāstā kyoṃ kara mile

kisako aba sijadoṃ kī hasarata kisako zoqa-e-bandagī
sara ke duśmana the sabhī jitane bhī saṅga-e-dara mile

unake hāthoṃ meṃ "qatīla" ika dina churī dekhoge tuma
vo munāfiqa jo gale lagakara tumheṃ aksara mile

✸ ✸ ✸

हम को अपनी पुरफ़िशानी.....

हम को अपनी पुरफ़िशानी[1] का सिला क्योंकर मिले
चाँद पर जाकर भी ऐ दुनिया हमें पत्थर मिले

सह्ने गुलशन का यह आलम था कि जब आंधी रुकी
हर तरफ़ बिखरे हुए कुछ तितलियों के पर मिले

रहबरों[2] के दम से अब राहों में इतनी भीड़ है
सोचते हैं अपने घर का रास्ता क्योंकर मिले

किसको अब सिजदों की हसरत किसको ज़ौक़–ए–बंदगी[3]
सर के दुश्मन थे सभी जितने भी संग–ए–दर[4] मिले

उनके हाथों में "क़तील" इक दिन छुरी देखोगे तुम
वो मुनाफ़िक़[5] जो गले लगकर तुम्हें अक्सर मिले

* * *

1. परिश्रम 2. रास्ता दिखाने वाले 3. उपासना का शौक़
4. पत्थर के द्वार (महबूब की चौखट) 5. बुरे आदमी

اندھیرے چھوڑ کر میں....

اندھیرے چھوڑ کر میں جا رہا تھا جب اُجالوں میں
کسی نے میرے ماتھے پر دیا بوسہ خیالوں میں

یقیناً ان کی سوچوں پر بڑھاپا چھا چکا ہوگا
اُلجھ کر رہ گئے جو لوگ ماضی کے حوالوں میں

بھڑکتے تھے کبھی جن میں گلابی آگ کے شعلے
بس اَب تو راکھ باقی رہ گئی ہے ان پیالوں میں

ہمیشہ گفتگو کر کے وہ شرمندہ ہوا مجھ سے
ملے اس کو سدا میرے جواب اپنے سوالوں میں

کھُلی آنکھوں میں قتیلؔ اس کو بھلا کب دیکھ سکتا ہوں
ملاقات اس سے اب ہوتی ہے خوابوں میں خیالوں میں

* * *

LEAVING DARKNESS.....

Leaving darkness behind, when I was heading for light
Someone, I thought, had kissed my forehead to delight

Surely their thinking would have fossilised
Who got enmeshed in the events of past flight

The urn from which purple flames were all leaping
Ashes only now remain, extinct in their plight

Beloved was always put to shame in conversation with me
As the questions put to me I answered forth right

I meet beloved in my dreams and in my thoughts
Far from me it be to catch beloved's sight

* * *

Aṃdhere Chod̂kar Maiṃ....

aṃdhere chod̂ara maiṃ jā rahā thā jaba ujāloṃ meṃ
kisī ne mere māthe para diyā bosā k͟hayāloṃ meṃ

yaqīnana unakī socoṃ para bud̂hāpā chā cukā hogā
ulajhakara raha gae jo loga māzī ke havāloṃ meṃ

bhad̂akate the kabhī jina meṃ gulābī āga ke śole
basa aba to rākha bāqī raha gaī hai una pyāloṃ meṃ

hameśā guftagū karake vo śarmindā huā mujha se
mile usako sadā mere javāba apane savāloṃ meṃ

khulī āṃkhoṃ "qatīla" usako bhalā kaba dekha sakatā hūm̐
mulāqāta usase aba hotī hai k͟hvāboṃ meṃ k͟hayāloṃ meṃ

अंधेरे छोड़कर मैं.....

अंधेरे छोड़कर मैं जा रहा था जब उजालों में
किसी ने मेरे माथे पर दिया बोसा ख्यालों में

यक़ीनन उनकी सोचों पर बुढ़ापा छा चुका होगा
उलझकर रह गए जो लोग माज़ी[1] के हवालों में

भड़कते थे कभी जिन में गुलाबी आग के शोले
बस अब तो राख बाक़ी रह गई है उन प्यालों में

हमेशा गुफ़्तगू[2] करके वो शर्मिंदा हुआ मुझ से
मिले उसको सदा मेरे जवाब अपने सवालों में

खुली आंखों "क़तील" उसको भला कब देख सकता हूँ
मुलाक़ात उससे अब होती है ख्वाबों में ख्यालों में

* * *

---

1. अतीत 2. बातचीत

کبھی نہ ختم ہوئیں....

کبھی نہ ختم ہوئیں گو شکایتیں اپنی
اُسی عروج پہ اب بھی ہیں چاہتیں اپنی

وہ دن گئے کہ تنک تر مزاج رکھتے تھے
تمہی نہیں تو کہاں کی عداوتیں اپنی

ہمیں تو فکر ہے اک دل کی اور محبت میں
شہنشہوں نے لُٹا دیں حکومتیں اپنی

وہ اِختلاف بڑھا قربتوں کے موسم میں
پڑوسیوں نے بدل لیں سکونتیں اپنی

تم اپنے حصّے کی پیتے تو جام کیوں چھِنتا
قتیلؔ سامنے آتی ہیں نیتیں اپنی

* * *

THOUGH OUR.....

Though our complaints never knew their end
Our love as well knew no bound for our friend

Gone are days when we were full of ego
If you are not around, who can we befriend

Our concern for heart apart, we should know for love
Kingdoms kings have sacrificed, for their right to fend

In the midst of friendship, differences so increased
That neighbours ill at ease, could not comprehend

You wouldn't lose your share of wine, if you were content
With your intent, O "Qateel", you might as well contend

* * *

Kabhī Na Khatm Huī....

kabhī na khatma huīṃ go śikāyateṃ apanī
usī urūja pe aba bhī haiṃ cāhateṃ apanī

vo dina gae ki tunaka tara mizāja rakhate the
tumhī nahīṃ to kahāṃ kī adāvateṃ apanī

hameṃ to fikra hai ika dila kī aura mohabbata meṃ
śahanśahoṃ ne luṭādīṃ hukūmateṃ apanī

vo ikhtilāfa baḋhā qurbatoṃ ke mausama meṃ
paḋosiyoṃ ne badala līṃ sukūnateṃ apanī

tuma apane hisase kī pīte to jāma kyoṃ chinatā
"qatīla" sāmane ātī haiṃ niyateṃ apanī

* * *

कभी न ख़त्म हुई.....

कभी न ख्त्म हुई गो शिकायतें अपनी
उसी उरूज[1] पे अब भी हैं चाहतें अपनी

वो दिन गए कि तुनक[2] तर मिज़ाज रखते थे
तुम्ही नहीं तो कहां की अदावतें[3] अपनी

हमें तो फ़िक्र है इक दिल की और मोहब्बत में
शहन्शहों ने लुटादीं हुकूमतें अपनी

वो इख़्तिलाफ़ बढ़ा क़ुर्बतों[4] के मौसम में
पड़ोसियों ने बदल लीं सुकूनतें[5] अपनी

तुम अपने हिस्से की पीते तो जाम क्यों छिनता
"क़तील" सामने आती हैं नियतें अपनी

* * *

1. ऊँचाई, शिखर 2. चिड़चिड़ाहट 3. दुश्मनी 4. क़रीब, पास रहने का मौसम 5. आवास, रिहाइश

شام کے سانولے چہرے....

شام کے سانولے چہرے کو نکھارا جائے
کیوں نہ ساغر سے کوئی چاند اُبھارا جائے

راس آیا نہیں تسکین کا ساحل کوئی
پھر مجھے پیاس کے دریا میں اُتارا جائے

اَب مرے شہر میں آئے گی سواری کس کی
اَب کِس امید پہ راہوں کو سنوارا جائے

مہرباں تیری نظر، تیری اَدائیں قاتل
تجھ کو کس نام سے اے دوست پکارا جائے

مجھ کو ڈر ہے ترے وعدے پہ بھروسہ کر کے
مفت میں یہ دلِ خوش فہم نہ مارا جائے

* * *

WE MIGHT WELL.....

We might well embellish evening's dark face
Why not refurbish goblet with moon's fulsome grace

I am not at all at home with the static coast
I wish again to merge with the ocean's base

Who will visit my habitat just to honour me
with what hope shall we decorate the place

Your glance is beguiling, your bearing is bewitching
Your beauty is, O friend, one hypnotic case

With my faith in your promise, I am so afraid
My trusting heart just may without any trace

* * *

Śām Ke Sām̐vle Cehre....

śāma ke sām̐vale cehare ko nikhārā jāe
kyoṃ na sāg̲hara se koī cām̐da ubhārā jāe

rāsa āyā nahīṃ taskīna kā sāhila koī
phira mujhe pyāsa ke dariyā meṃ utārā jāe

aba mire śahara meṃ āegī savārī kisakī
aba kisa ummīda pe rāhoṃ ko saṃvārā jāe

meharabāṃ terī nazara terī adāaiṃ qātila
tujha ko kisa nāma se ai dosta pukārā jāe

mujha ko ḍara hai tire vāde pe bharosā karake
mufta meṃ yaha dila-e-k̲h̲uśa-fahma na mārā jāe

* * *

शाम के साँवले चेहरे.....

शाम के साँवले चेहरे को निखारा जाए
क्यों न साग़र[1] से कोई चाँद उभारा जाए

रास आया नहीं तस्कीन का साहिल कोई
फिर मुझे प्यास के दरिया में उतारा जाए

अब मिरे शहर में आएगी सवारी किसकी
अब किस उम्मीद पे राहों को संवारा जाए

मेहरबां तेरी नज़र तेरी अदाऐं क़ातिल
तुझ को किस नाम से ऐ दोस्त पुकारा जाए

मुझ को डर है तिरे वादे पे भरोसा करके
मुफ़्त में यह दिल-ए-खुश-फ़ह्म[2] न मारा जाए

✸ ✸ ✸

---

1. जाम 2. झूठी आशाएं बांधने वाला

یوں لگے دوست....

یوں لگے دوست ترا مجھ سے خفا ہو جانا
جس طرح پھول سے خوشبو کا جدا ہو جانا

اہلِ دل سے یہ ترا ترکِ تعلّق یعنی
وقت سے پہلے اسیروں کا رِہا ہو جانا

یوں اگر ہو تو جہاں میں کوئی کافر نہ رہے
معجزہ ہے ترے وعدے کا وفا ہو جانا

زندگی میں بھی چلوں گا ترے پیچھے پیچھے
تو مرے دوست کا نقشِ کفِ پا ہو جانا

جانے یہ کون سی کیفیتِ غمخواری ہے
میرے پیتے ہی قتیلؔ اس کو نشہ ہو جانا

* * *

I REGARD YOUR ANGST.....

I regard your angst against me, O friend
As if the scent against its flower to offend

To break of relations with your own admirers
Is to send your captives on parole's end

Fulfilment of your promise is nothing short miracle
None in the world to doubt or to apprehend

I shall follow you resolutely in my life's passage
For your footprints absolutely, I wish you condescend

What is the strange sense of sympathy, O "Qateel"
Beloved is impressed before a word of mouth I send

* * *

Yūm̐ Lage Dost....

yūm̐ lage dosta tirā mujhase k͟hafā ho jānā
jisa taraha phūla se k͟huśbū kā judā ho jānā

ahle dila se ye tirā tarka-e-taalluqa yānī
vaqta se pahale asīroṃ kā rihā ho jānā

yūm̐ agara ho to jahāṃ meṃ koī kāfira na rahe
mojazā hai tire vāde kā vafā ho jānā

zindagī maiṃ bhī calūṅgā tire pīche-pīche
tū mire dosta kā naqśa-e-kafa-e-pā ho jānā

jāne vo kaunasī kaifiyata-e-g͟hama k͟hvārī hai
mere pīte hī "qatīla" usako naśā ho jānā

✹ ✹ ✹

यूँ लगे दोस्त.....

यूँ लगे दोस्त तिरा मुझसे ख़फ़ा हो जाना
जिस तरह फूल से ख़ुश्बू का जुदा हो जाना

अह्ले दिल से ये तिरा तर्क-ए-तअल्लुक़[1] यानी
वक़्त से पहले असीरों[2] का रिहा हो जाना

यूँ अगर हो तो जहां में कोई काफ़िर न रहे
मोजज़ा[3] है तिरे वादे का वफ़ा हो जाना

ज़िंदगी मैं भी चलूंगा तिरे पीछे-पीछे
तू मिरे दोस्त का नक़्श-ए-कफ़-ए-पा[4] हो जाना

जाने वो कौनसी कैफ़ियत-ए-ग़म ख़्वारी[5] है
मेरे पीते ही "क़तील" उसको नशा हो जाना

* * *

1. सम्बन्ध-विच्छेद 2. कैदी 3. चमत्कार 4. पद-चिन्ह
5. सहानुभूति

ترس رہا ہوں میں....

ترس رہا ہوں میں تو اپنے پیاروں کو
دنیا گھر کہتی ہے کچھ دیواروں کو

پیارے لوگوں سے جو پیار نہیں کرتے
کیسے میں سمجھاؤں اُن بے چاروں کو

گرم گلابی آنچ سہی رخساروں کو
پھول سمجھ کر چھولو اِن انگاروں کو

گھر والو! جب گھر میں چوری ہو جائے
سب سے پہلے پکڑو پہرے داروں کو

دیکھ کے اس کو بڑے بڑے فنکار قتیلؔ
بھُول گئے اپنے شہکاروں کو

* * *

I LONG FOR MY LOVED.....

I long for my loved ones indeed
More than brick and mortar a house is indeed

Those who love not beautiful folk
Good advice how will they heed

Even if cheeks are purple hot
Touch these embers as if flower weed

In case of theft, O inhabitants of citadel
First question the sentinels for their creed

Seeing beloved, many masters of art
Just forgot their own creative creed

* * *

Taras Rahā Hūm̐ Maiṃ....

tarasa rahā hūm̐ maiṃ to apane pyāroṃ ko
duniyā ghara kahatī hai kucha dīvāroṃ ko

pyāre logoṃ se jo pyāra nahīṃ karate
kaise maiṃ samajhāum̐ una be cāroṃ ko

narma gulābī ām̐ca sahī rukhasāroṃ kī
phūla samajha kara chū lo una aṃgāroṃ ko

ghara vālā! jaba ghara meṃ corī ho jāe
sabase pahale pakaḍo paharedāroṃ ko

dekhake usako baḍe-baḍe fanakāra "qatīla"
bhūla gae apane-apane śahakāroṃ ko

* * *

तरस रहा हूँ मैं.....

तरस रहा हूँ मैं तो अपने प्यारों को
दुनिया घर कहती है कुछ दीवारों को

प्यारे लोगों से जो प्यार नहीं करते
कैसे मैं समझाऊँ उन बे चारों को

नर्म गुलाबी आँच सही रुख़सारों की
फूल समझ कर छू लो उन अंगारों को

घर वालो! जब घर में चोरी हो जाए
सबसे पहले पकड़ो पहरेदारों को

देखके उसको बड़े-बड़े फ़नकार "क़तील"
भूल गए अपने-अपने शहकारों[1] को

* * *

1. कला कृतियां

لوگوں میں احتیاط....

لوگوں میں احتیاط کا پیکر بنا رہا
وہ میرا نام سُن کے بھی پتھر بنا رہا

کھولی بیاضِ عمر تو آنکھوں میں دیر تک
یادوں کی چاند رات کا منظر بنا رہا

حالات بار بار مٹاتے نہیں کسے؟
میں ساری عمر حرفِ مکرّر بنا رہا

جب تک درندگی کی ہوائیں چلی نہ تھیں
سنسان جنگلوں میں مرا گھر بنا رہا

کیسے نہ دوں قتیلؔ دُعا اس کے حُسن کو
میں جس پہ شعر کہہ کے سخنور بنا رہا

* * *

AMONG PEOPLE.....

Among people, beloved was circumspect
Even hearing my name did not react

Opening book of life recalled the past
Nightlong, memories made their own impact

Worldly woes spare no one ever
They obliterated all my life's aspect

As long as rule of law had prevailed
Peace I had availed with the jungle's pact

Why not, O "Qateel", I sing beloved's praises
Writing verses for beloved made me a poet perfect

* * *

Logoṃ Meṃ Ehtiyāt....

logoṃ meṃ ehatiyāta kā paikara banā rahā
vo merā nāma sunake bhī patthara banā rahā

kholī byāza-e-umra to āṁkhoṃ meṃ dera taka
yādoṃ kī cāṁda rāta kā mañzara banā rahā

hālāta bāra-bāra miṭate nahīṃ kise?
maiṃ sārī umra harfa-e-mukarrara banā rahā

jaba taka darindagī kī havāeṃ calī na thīṃ
sunasāna jaṅgaloṃ meṃ mirā ghara banā rahā

kaise na dūṃ "qatīla" duā usake husna ko
maiṃ jisa pe śera kaha ke sukhanavara banā rahā

* * *

लोगों में एहतियात.....

लोगों में एहतियात का पैकर[1] बना रहा
वो मेरा नाम सुनके भी पत्थर बना रहा

खोली ब्याज़-ए-उम्र[2] तो आँखों में देर तक
यादों की चाँद रात का मंज़र बना रहा

हालात बार-बार मिटते नहीं किसे?
मैं सारी उम्र हर्फ़-ए-मुकर्रर[3] बना रहा

जब तक दरिंदगी की हवाएं चली न थीं
सुनसान जंगलों में मिरा घर बना रहा

कैसे न दूं "क़तील" दुआ उसके हुस्न को
मैं जिस पे शेर कह के सुख़नवर[4] बना रहा

* * *

---

1. सतर्कता की मूरत 2. जीवन पुस्तक 3. बार-बार दोहराया जाने वाला शब्द 4. शायर

لکھ دوں جو سراپا....

لکھ دوں جو سراپا کسی بے پنکھ پری کا!
سب شہر میں چرچا ہو مری نغمہ گری کا!

بُجھتی ہوئی ہر سانس میں جل جاتی ہیں شمعیں
آئے مرے ہونٹوں پہ جونہی نام کسی کا

دہرائے چلا جاتا ہے پی پی کی صدائیں
پیغام نہ لایا ہو پپیہا مرے پی کا

بکھراتی ہے جب گھور اندھیرے شب ہجراں
ماتھے پہ سجالیتے ہیں وہ چاند کا ٹیکا

روکے ہیں قتیلؔ اشک تو دو شعر ہی کہہ لے
کچھ بوجھ تو ہلکا ہو مری جاں ترے جی کا

* * *

IF I WRITE ABOUT.....

If I write about some wingless fairy incarnate
My verses the whole world will come to appreciate

In every dying breath, it breathes a new life
Beloved's name on my lips even as I state

The nightingal repeatedly is uttering beloved's name
Beloved's message it has brought surely to stimulate

When night of separation is enveloped in darkness
Beloved is feigning elsewhere with moon to decorate

Write some verses, O "Qateel", to assuage your tears
So your mind is lightened, not to agitate

* * *

Likh Dūm̐ Jo Sarāpā....

likha dūm̐ jo sarāpā kisī be paṅkha parī kā
saba śahara meṃ carcā ho mirī nag̲hamā garī kā

bujhatī huī hara sāṃsa meṃ jala jātī haiṃ śamaaiṃ
āe mire hoṇṭoṃ pe jyoṃ hī nāma kisī kā

doharāe calā jātā hai pī-pī kī sadāeṃ
paig̲hāma na lāyā ho papīha mire pī kā

bikharātī hai jaba ghora aṃdhere śaba-e-hijarām̐
māthe pe sajā lete haiṃ vo cām̐da kā ṭīkā

roke haiṃ, "qatīla" aśka to do śera hī kahale
kucha bojha to halkā ho mirī jāṃ tire jī kā

* * *

लिख दूँ जो सरापा.....

लिख दूँ जो सरापा किसी बे पंख परी का
सब शहर में चर्चा हो मिरी नग़मा गरी[1] का

बुझती हुई हर सांस में जल जाती हैं शमऐं
आए मिरे होंटों पे ज्यों ही नाम किसी का

दोहराए चला जाता है पी–पी की सदाएं
पैग़ाम न लाया हो पपीहा मिरे पी का

बिखराती है जब घोर अंधेरे शब–ए–हिजराँ[2]
माथे पे सजा लेते हैं वो चाँद का टीका

रोके हैं "क़तील" अश्क तो दो शेर ही कहले
कुछ बोझ तो हल्का हो मिरी जां तिरे जी का

* * *

1. गीत कारी 2. जुदाई की रात

طوفاں کوئی اُٹھے....

طوفاں کوئی اُٹھے نہ مرے احتجاج سے
ڈرتا ہوں تیرے شہر کے رسم و رواج سے

کہتے ہیں ایک شخص نے کرلی ہی خودکشی
وہ انتقام لینے چلا تھا سماج سے

لینا پڑے گا عشق میں ترکِ وفا سے کام
پرہیز اس مرض میں ہے بہتر علاج سے

جی چاہے اس کی راہگزر میں کھڑے رہیں
اس عاشقی میں ہم تو گئے کام کاج سے

کوئی نشے میں سچ کو چھپاتا نہیں قتیلؔ
شامل ہوں میں بھی حلقۂ رنداں میں آج سے

* * *

LET NO ONE TAKE.....

Let no one take umbrage at my protest
My etiquette, regretfully , may not be at its best

As it is rumoured, someone has taken his life
He had wished to avenge himself the society's neglect

Prevention is said to be better than cure itself
If fidelity is lacking in the love's quest

In the love pursuit we are all bereft
Heart wishes it may remain at beloved's behest

One cannot conceal the truth, intoxicated, O "Qateel"
To day I ride the wine wagon, not without zest

* * *

Tūfāṃ Koī Uṭhe....

tūfāṃ koī uṭhe na mire ehatijāja se
ḍaratā hūm̐ tere śahra ke rasma-o-rivāja se

kahate haiṃ eka śakhsa ne karalī hai khudakuśī
vo inteqāma lene calā thā samāja se

lenā paḍegā iśqa meṃ tarka-e-vafā se kāma
paraheza isa maraza meṃ hai behatara ilāja se

jī cāhe usakī rāhaguzara meṃ khaḍe raheṃ
isa aāśiqī meṃ hama to gae kāma-kāja se

koī naśe meṃ saca ko chipātā nahīṃ "qatīla"
śāmila hūm̐ maiṃ bhī halqā-e-rindām̐ meṃ āja se

* * *

तूफ़ां कोई उठे.....

तूफ़ां कोई उठे न मिरे एहतिजाज[1] से
डरता हूँ तेरे शह्‌र के रस्म-ओ-रिवाज से

कहते हैं एक शख़्स ने करली है ख़ुदकुशी[2]
वो इन्तक़ाम[3] लेने चला था समाज से

लेना पड़ेगा इश्क़ में तर्क-ए-वफ़ा[4] से काम
परहेज़ इस मरज़ में है बेहतर इलाज से

जी चाहे उसकी राहगुज़र में खड़े रहें
इस आशिक़ी में हम तो गए काम-काज से

कोई नशे में सच को छिपाता नहीं "क़तील"
शामिल हूँ मैं भी हल्क़ा-ए-रिन्दाँ[5] में आज से

* * *

---

1. प्रतिवाद 2. आत्महत्या 3. बदला 4. वफ़ा छोड़ना 5. शराब पीने वालों की सभा

زندگی کی دلدل ہے....

زندگی کی دلدل ہے اور ناتواں انساں
دامِ خاک سے بچ کر جائیگا کہاں انساں

دھوپ بن کے چمکا ہے، برف بن کے پگھلے گا
صورتیں بدلتا ہے، زیرِ آسماں انساں

شام تک تو شعلہ تھا، اُس کے بعد کیا کہیے
رات جب پڑی شبنم، بن گیا دھواں انساں

اُس نے لوحِ فردا پر، لکھنا چاہا نام اپنا
بَن کے رہ گیا لیکن، یادِ رفتگاں انساں

گو قتیلؔ قدموں سے بے بسی بھی لپٹی ہے
پھر بھی راہِ ہستی میں ہے رواں دواں انساں

* * *

MAN IS WEEK AGAINST.....

Man is weak against the life's quagmire
How man will escape earth's dragnet entire

Sometimes it is blazing sun, sometimes frigid snow
Man assumes many forms and different attire

When nightly dew fell, man became mellow
Till dusk, though, he was flaming all fire

On the history's tablet, he wanted to inscribe his name
But man became a relic of the history prior

O "Qateel", though man is fated hapless and helpless
Still from the trek of life, man does not retire

* * *

Zindagī Kī Daldal Hai....

zindagī kī daladala hai aura nātavāṃ iṃsām̐
dāma-e-khāka se bacakara jāegā kahāṃ iṃsām̐

dhūpa banake camakā hai, barfa banake pighalegā
sūrateṃ badalatā hai zera-e-āsamāṃ iṃsām̐

śāma taka to śolā thā, usake bāda kyā kahie
rāta jaba paḍī śabanama bana gayā dhuāṃ iṃsām̐

usane lauha-e-fardā para likhanā cāhā nāma apanā
banake raha gayā lekina yāda-e-raftagām̐ iṃsām̐

go "qatīla" qadamoṃ se bebasī bhī lipaṭī hai
phira bhī rāha-e-hastī meṃ hai ravāṃ-davāṃ iṃsām̐

* * *

ज़िंदगी की दलदल है.....

ज़िंदगी की दलदल है और नातवां[1] इंसाँ
दाम-ए-ख़ाक[2] से बचकर जाएगा कहां इंसाँ

धूप बनके चमका है, बर्फ़ बनके पिघलेगा
सूरतें बदलता है ज़ेर-ए-आसमां इंसाँ

शाम तक तो शोला था, उसके बाद क्या कहिए
रात जब पड़ी शबनम बन गया धुआं इंसाँ

उसने लौह-ए-फ़र्दा[3] पर लिखना चाहा नाम अपना
बनके रह गया लेकिन याद-ए-रफ़्तगाँ[4] इंसाँ

गो "क़तील" क़दमों से बेबसी भी लिपटी है
फिर भी राह-ए-हस्ती[5] में है रवां-दवां[6] इंसाँ

* * *

1. कमज़ोर 2. मिट्टी का जाल 3. कल का पट 4. बीते समय की याद 5. जीवनपथ 6. चलता फिरता, गतिशील

شام نظارہ...

شام نظارہ کو تاحدِّ سحر جانے دیا
تھا ہمیں انجام کا دھڑکا مگر جانے دیا

کچھ نہیں تو صرف خالی جام ہی کھنکائیں گے
محتسب نے سُوئے میخانہ اگر جانے دیا

پیار کرنے کو جو مانگا اور ہم نے اک جنم
زندگی نے مسکرا کر ہم کو مرجانے دیا

الجھنیں کچھ اور بھی میری بڑھانے کے لئے
نصف شب کے بعد اُس نے مجھ کو گھر جانے دیا

میں ہی مقتل میں وہ غیرت مند انساں تھا قتیلؔ
آن اپنی جس نے رکھ لی اور سر جانے دیا

* * *

FROM DUSK TO DAWN.....

From dusk to dawn, we let our eyes be satiated
Though afraid of end, we all along waited

If nothing else, we'll play with empty goblets
If the tavern sentinel allows us to be sedated

We begged for another birth for another love
Life was indulgent, let us be terminated

To add to my woes, beloved let me go
At the midnight hour, woes not mitigated

In the skirmish of love, I was the only one
O "Qateel", who did not let his honour be decimated

* * *

Śām-E-Zzārā....

śāma-e-nazzārā ko tā hadda-e-sahara jāne diyā
thā hameṃ aṃjāma kā dhaḋakā magara jāne diyā

kucha nahīṃ to sirfa k̲h̲ālī jāma hī khankāeṃge
mohtasiba ne sū-e-mayak̲h̲ānā agara jāne diyā

pyāra karane ko jo māṅgā aura hamane ika janama
zindagī ne muskarākara hamako mara jāne diyā

ulajhaneṃ kucha aura bhī merī baḋhāne ke lie
nisfa śaba ke bāda usane mujhako ghara jāne diyā

maiṃ hī maqatala meṃ vo g̲h̲airata manda iṃsām̐ thā "qatila"
āna apanī jisane rakha lī aura sara jāne diyā

* * *

शाम-ए-नज़ारा.....

शाम–ए–नज़्ज़ारा[1] को ता हद्द–ए–सहर[2] जाने दिया
था हमें अंजाम का धड़का मगर जाने दिया

कुछ नहीं तो सिर्फ़ खाली जाम ही खन्काएंगे
मोह्तसिब[3] ने सू–ए–मयखाना अगर जाने दिया

प्यार करने को जो मांगा और हमने इक जनम
ज़िन्दगी ने मुस्कराकर हमको मर जाने दिया

उलझनें कुछ और भी मेरी बढ़ाने के लिए
निस्फ़ शब[4] के बाद उसने मुझको घर जाने दिया

मैं ही मक़तल[5] में वो ग़ैरत मंद इंसाँ था "क़तील"
आन अपनी जिसने रख ली और सर जाने दिया

✹ ✹ ✹

---

1. शाम का दृश्य 2. सुबह की सीमा तक 3. धर्म प्रचारक
4. आधी रात 5. जहां हत्या की जाती है

کیا عشق تھا....

کیا عشق تھا جو باعثِ رسوائی بن گیا
یارو تمام شہر تماشائی بن گیا

بِن مانگے مِل گئے مری آنکھوں کو رَت جگے
میں جب سے ایک چاند کا شیدائی بن گیا

دیکھا جو اس کا دستِ حنائی قریب سے
احساس گونجتی ہوئی شہنائی بن گیا

کرتا رہا جو روز مجھے اُس سے بَدگماں
وہ شخص بھی اب اُس کا تمنّائی بن گیا

وہ تیری بھی تو پہلی محبت نہ تھی قتیلؔ
پھر کیا ہوا اگر کوئی ہرجائی بن گیا

* * *

WHAT WAS THAT LOVE.....

What was that love which led to our shame
Among the whole populace, a spectacle we became

Ever since I was enamoured of beloved
My eyes have lost their sleep in the love game

As I saw from near beloved's manicured hands
I was thrilled to bits, nervous all the same

The person who had urged me against my beloved
He was in the process to become so tame

So what O "Qateel", if beloved was so fickle
This was not, in your case, your very first flame

* * *

Kyā Iśq Thā....

kyā iśqa thā jo bāisa-e-rusvāī bana gayā
yāro tamāma śahra tamāśāī bana gayā

bina māṅge mila gae mirī āṃkhoṃ ko ratajage
maiṃ jaba se eka cāँda kā śaidāī bana gayā

dekhā jo usakā dasta-e-hināī qarība se
ehasāsa gūñjatī huī śahanāī bana gayā

karatā rahā jo roza mujhe usase badagumāṃ
vo śak̲h̲sa bhī aba usakā tamannāī bana gayā

vo terī bhī to pahalī mohabbata na thī "qatīla"
phira kyā huā agara koī harajāī bana gayā

* * *

क्या इश्क़ था.....

क्या इश्क़ था जो बाइस–ए–रुस्वाई[1] बन गया
यारो तमाम शहर तमाशाई बन गया

बिन मांगे मिल गए मिरी आंखों को रतजगे
मैं जब से एक चाँद का शैदाई[2] बन गया

देखा जो उसका दस्त–ए–हिनाई[3] क़रीब से
एहसास गूंजती हुई शहनाई बन गया

करता रहा जो रोज़ मुझे उससे बदगुमां
वो शख्स भी अब उसका तमन्नाई बन गया

वो तेरी भी तो पहली मोहब्बत न थी "क़तील"
फिर क्या हुआ अगर कोई हरजाई बन गया

* * *

---

1. बदनामी का कारण 2. आशिक़ 3. मेंहदी रचे हाथ

میں نے پوچھا....

میں نے پوچھا، پہلا پتھر مجھ پر کون اٹھائے گا
آئی اک آواز کہ تو جس کا محسنؔ کہلائے گا

ڈالی ہے اِس خوش فہمی نے عادت مجھ کو سونے کی
نکلے گا جب سورج تو خود مجھ کو آن جگائے گا

لوگو میرے ساتھ چلو تم جو کچھ ہے وہ آگے ہے
پیچھے مڑکر دیکھنے والا پتھر کا ہو جائے گا

میرے بعد وفا کا دھوکا اور کسی سے مت کرنا
گالی دے گی دُنیا تجھ کو، سر میرا جھک جائے گا

سُوکھ گئی جب اُن آنکھوں میں پیار کی نیلی جھیل قتیلؔ
تیرے درد کا زرد سمندر کا ہے شور مچائے گا

* * *

I HAD WONDERED.....

I had wondered who will cast the first stone
Came the voice, someone for whom favours had been shown

I go to sound sleep with this fond belief
That the rising sun will not let me all alone

O friend, come with me to look for the future
Beckoning the past will take you to the age of stone

Don't ensnare after me with your promise of fealty
The whole world will blame you, for me to atone

O "Qateel", when beloved's eyes are dried of love
Why at all you may cry and bemoan

* * *

Maiṁne Pūchā...

mainne pūchā, pahalā patthara mujha para kauna uṭhāegā?
āī ika āvāza ki tū jisakā muhasina kahalāegā

ḍālī hai isa khuśa fahmī ne ādata mujhako sone kī
nikalegā jaba sūraja to khuda mujha ko āna jagāegā

logoṃ mere sātha calo tuma jo kucha hai vo āge hai
pīche muḍakara dekhane vālā patthara kā ho jāegā

mere bāda vafā kā dhokhā aura kisī se mata karanā
gālī degī duniyā tujhako sara merā jhuka jāegā

sūkha gaī jaba una āṃkhoṃ meṃ pyāra kī nīlī jhīla "qatīla"
tere darda kā zarda samandara kāhe śora macāegā

* * *

मैंने पूछा,.....

मैंने पूछा, पहला पत्थर मुझ पर कौन उठाएगा?
आई इक आवाज़ कि तू जिसका मुहसिन[1] कहलाएगा

डाली है इस खुश फ़हमी ने आदत मुझको सोने की
निकलेगा जब सूरज तो खुद मुझ को आन जगाएगा

लोगो मेरे साथ चलो तुम जो कुछ है वो आगे है
पीछे मुड़कर देखने वाला पत्थर का हो जाएगा

मेरे बाद वफ़ा का धोखा और किसी से मत करना
गाली देगी दुनिया तुझको सर मेरा झुक जाएगा

सूख गई जब उन आंखों में प्यार की नीली झील "क़तील"
तेरे दर्द का ज़र्द[2] समन्दर काहे शोर मचाएगा

* * *

1. परोपकारी 2. पीला

تجھے بھی ڈر ہے کسی کا....

تجھے بھی ڈر ہے کسی کا تو دُور سے پڑھ لے
لکھی ہوئی ہے دلوں کی پُکار چہروں پر

لگی ہے آگ یہ کیسی وفا کے جنگل میں
جلا کے رکھ دیئے کس نے چنار چہروں پر

وَفا کی کھوج میں نِکلو تو پاؤں جلتے ہیں
ابھی تو صرف جَما ہے غُبار چہروں پر

میں تیری بزم میں کِس کِس کی دشمنی لیتا
لکھا تھا نام ترا بے شمار چہروں پر

مری نظر تو ہے پھر بھی مری نظر یارو
اب آئینوں کو نہیں اعتبار چہروں پر

* * *

IF YOU ARE AFRAID.....

If you are afraid, read it from afar
That the scars of heart are engraved on the face

What fire has engulfed the whole fealty forest
That trees as well as woods are denuded of their base

In the search for fealty, feet become sore
Yet this is just the beginning, as a book's preface

Not to incur the enmity of people in your enclave
They are your admirers under your spell and grace

Not to reckon, O friends, with my view alone
Mirrors now no longer trust anyone's face

* * *

Tujhe Bhī Ḍara Hai Kisī Kā...

tujhe bhī ḍara hai kisī kā to dūra se paḍha le
likhī huī hai diloṃ kī pukāra ceharoṃ para

lagī hai āga ye kaisī vafā ke jaṅgala meṃ
jalā ke rakha die kisa ne cunāra ceharoṃ para

vafā kī khoja meṃ nikalo to pāṃva jalate haiṃ
abhī to sirfa jamā hai g͟hubāra ceharoṃ para

maiṃ terī bazma meṃ kisa-kisa kī duśmanī letā
likhā thā nāma tirā beśumāra ceharoṃ para

mirī nazara to hai phira bhī mirī nazara yāro
aba āīnoṃ ko nahīṃ etabāra ceharoṃ para

✸ ✸ ✸

तुझे भी डर है किसी का.....

तुझे भी डर है किसी का तो दूर से पढ़ ले
लिखी हुई है दिलों की पुकार चेहरों पर

लगी है आग ये कैसी वफ़ा के जंगल में
जला के रख दिए किस ने चनार चेहरों पर

वफ़ा की खोज में निकलो तो पांव जलते हैं
अभी तो सिर्फ़ जमा है गुबार[1] चेहरों पर

मैं तेरी बज़्म[2] में किस-किस की दुश्मनी लेता
लिखा था नाम तिरा बेशुमार[3] चेहरों पर

मिरी नज़र तो है फिर भी मिरी नज़र यारो
अब आईनों को नहीं एतबार चेहरों पर

* * *

---

1. धूल 2. महफ़िल 3. अनगिनत

صدمہ تو ہے مجھے....

صدمہ تو ہے مجھے بھی کہ تجھ سے جُدا ہوں میں
لیکن یہ سوچتا ہوں کہ اب تیرا کیا ہوں میں

میں خودکشی کے جرم کا کرتا ہوں اعتراف
اپنے بدن کی قبر میں کب سے گڑا ہوں میں

کس کس کا نام لاؤں زباں پر کہ تیرے ساتھ
ہر روز ایک شخص نیا دیکھتا ہوں میں

کیا جانے کس ادا سے لیا تو نے میرا نام
دنیا سمجھ رہی ہے کہ سب کچھ ترا ہوں میں

جاگا ہوا ضمیر وہ آئینہ ہے قتیلؔ
سونے سے پہلے روز جسے دیکھتا ہوں میں

* * *

I AM ALSO SHOCKED.....

I am also shocked that from you I am separated
But still I keep wondering how we are related

I confess to the crime of committing suicide
With in my body's grave I am incarcerated

Who all I may mention along with your name
I see a person new with you, daily integrated

With such endearing style you have mentioned my name
In the eyes of the world, I am fully elevated

My well awake conscience acts like a mirror
O "Qateel", I view it daily and feel exonerated

* * *

Sadmā To Hai Mujhe...

sadamā to hai mujhe bhī ki tujhase judā hūm̐ maiṃ
lekina ye socatā hūm̐ ki aba terā kyā hūm̐ maiṃ

maiṃ <u>kh</u>udakuśī ke jurma kā karatā hūm̐ aitarāfa
apane badana kī qabra meṃ kaba se gaḍā hūm̐ maiṃ

kisa-kisa kā nāma lāum̐ zabāṃ para ki tere sātha
hara roza eka śa<u>kh</u>sa nayā dekhatā hūm̐ maiṃ

kyā jāne kisa adā se liyā tūne merā nāma
duniyā samajha rahī hai ki saba kucha terā hūm̐ maiṃ

jāgā huā zamīra vo āīnā hai "qatīla"
sone se pahale roza jise dekhatā hūm̐ maiṃ

✸ ✸ ✸

सदमा तो है मुझे.....

सदमा तो है मुझे भी कि तुझसे जुदा हूँ मैं
लेकिन ये सोचता हूँ कि अब तेरा क्या हूँ मैं

मैं खुदकुशी के जुर्म का करता हूँ ऐतराफ़[1]
अपने बदन की क़ब्र में कब से गड़ा हूँ मैं

किस–किस का नाम लाऊँ ज़बां पर कि तेरे साथ
हर रोज़ एक शख्स नया देखता हूँ मैं

क्या जाने किस अदा से लिया तूने मेरा नाम
दुनिया समझ रही है कि सब कुछ तिरा हूँ मैं

जागा हुआ ज़मीर[2] वो आईना है "क़तील"
सोने से पहले रोज़ जिसे देखता हूँ मैं

* * *

1. स्वीकारोक्ति 2. अन्तरात्मा

مرحلہ رات کا....

مرحلہ رات کا جب آئے گا
جسم سائے کو ترس جائے گا

اعتبار اس کا ہمیشہ کرنا
وہ تو جھوٹی بھی قسم کھائے گا

تو نہ ہو گی تو پھر اے شامِ فراق
کون آ کر ہمیں بہلائے گا

ہم اسے یاد بہت آئیں گے
جب اُسے بھی کوئی ٹھکرائے گا

کائنات اس کی مری ذات میں ہے
مجھ کو کھو کر وہ کسے پائے گا

٭ ٭ ٭

WHEN NIGHT.....

When night will descend around
Shadow with the body will not be found

Trust your beloved all the time
Even though false promises around

O night of separation without you
Who else will amuse us and confound

When beloved will be jilted by someone
Beloved's remorse will know no bound

Losing me what will beloved gain
As beloved's universe with me is bound

* * *

Marhalā Rāt Kā....

marahalā rāta kā jaba āegā
jisma sāe ko tarasa jāegā

etabāra usakā hameśā karanā
vo to jhūṭhī bhī qasama khāegā

tū na hogī to phira ai śāma-e-firāqa
kauna ākara hameṃ bahalāegā

hama use yāda bahuta āeṃge
jaba use bhī koī ṭhukarāegā

kāyanāta usakī mirī zāta meṃ hai
mujha ko khokara vo kise pāegā

* * *

मरहला[1] रात का.....

मरहला[1] रात का जब आएगा
जिस्म साए को तरस जाएगा

एतबार उसका हमेशा करना
वो तो झूठी भी क़सम खाएगा

तू न होगी तो फिर ऐ शाम–ए–फ़िराक़
कौन आकर हमें बहलाएगा

हम उसे याद बहुत आएंगे
जब उसे भी कोई ठुकराएगा

कायनात उसकी मिरी ज़ात में है
मुझ को खोकर वो किसे पाएगा

* * *

1. मुक़ाम, पड़ाव

میں سمندر بھی ہوں....

میں سمندر بھی ہوں موتی بھی ہوں، غوطہ زن بھی
کوئی بھی نام مرا لے کے بُلالے مجھ کو

تو نے دیکھا نہیں آئینے سے آگے کچھ بھی
خود پرستی میں کہیں تو نہ گنوالے مجھ کو

کل کی بات اور ہے، میں اَب سا رہوں یا نہ رہوں
جتنا جی چاہے ترا، آج ستالے مجھ کو

خود کو میں بانٹ نہ ڈالوں کہیں دامن دامن
کردیا تو نے اگر میرے حوالے مجھ کو

بادہ پھر بادہ ہے، میں زہر بھی پی جاؤں قتیلؔ
شرط یہ ہے، کوئی باہوں میں سنبھالے مجھ کو

* * *

I AM ALSO AN OCEAN.....

I am also an ocean, also pearl, also pearl diver
Let any one beckon me, with any name

You didn't see anything beyond the mirrors surface
In your self esteem you may lose your fame

You may torment as much as you like to day
Tomorrow is another day, I may not be the same

I may pull myself apart thread bear thread by thread
If upon my body and soul I lay any claim

Wine is wine, I may partake even poisonous potion
If only beloved will own me and acclaim

* * *

Maiṃ Samandar Bhī Hūm̐...

maiṃ samandara bhī hūm̐, motī bhī hūm̐, g̲hotā-zana bhī
koī bhī nāma mirā leke bulāle mujhako

tūne dekhā nahīṃ āīne se āge kucha bhī
k̲hudaparastī meṃ kahīṃ tū na gam̐vā le mujhako

kala kī bāta aura hai, maiṃ aba sā rahūm̐ yā na rahūm̐
jitanā jī cāhe tirā, āja satāle mujhako

k̲huda ko maiṃ bām̐ṭa na ḍālūm̐ kahīṃ dāmana-dāmana
kara diyā tūne agara mere havāle mujhako

bādā phira bādā hai maiṃ zahara bhī pī jāuṃ "qatīla"
śarta ye hai, koī bāhoṃ meṃ sambhāle mujhako

* * *

मैं समंदर भी हूँ.....

मैं समंदर भी हूँ, मोती भी हूँ, ग़ोता-ज़न[1] भी
कोई भी नाम मिरा लेके बुलाले मुझको

तूने देखा नहीं आईने से आगे कुछ भी
खुदपरस्ती[2] में कहीं तू न गँवा ले मुझको

कल की बात और है, मैं अब सा रहूँ या न रहूँ
जितना जी चाहे तिरा, आज सताले मुझको

खुद को मैं बाँट न डालूं कहीं दामन-दामन
कर दिया तूने अगर मेरे हवाले मुझको

बादा[3] फिर बादा है मैं ज़हर भी पी जाऊं "क़तील"
शर्त ये है, कोई बाहों में संभाले मुझको

✸ ✸ ✸

1. ग़ोताख़ोर 2. स्वयं की पूजा 3. शराब

جو بھی غنچہ ترے....

جو بھی غنچہ ترے ہونٹوں پہ کِھلا کرتا ہے
وہ مری تنگئ داماں کا گِلا کرتا ہے

دیر سے آج مرا سَر ہے ترے زانو پر
یہ وہ رتبہ ہے جو شاہوں کو مِلا کرتا ہے

میں تو بیٹھا ہوں دبائے ہوئے طوفانوں کو
تو مرے دل کے دھڑکنے کا گِلا کرتا ہے

رات یوں چاند کو دیکھا ہے ندی میں رقصاں
جیسے جھُومر ترے ماتھے پہ ہلا کرتا ہے

کون کافر تجھے الزامِ تغافل دے گا
جو بھی کرتا ہے محبت سے گِلا کرتا ہے

* * *

EVERY SMILE.....

Every smile on your lips helps to explain
Your lack of pleasure for me and disdain

I am resting long my head on your shoulder
This is a signal honour which kings may attain

I am suppressing within myself many a thousand storm
Why my heart is agitated, you want to complain

I saw the moon aquiver in the river tonight
Like jewels on your forehead to shine and to wane

They do in good faith to complain against neglect
Whoever in the world would any doubt entertain

* * *

Jo Bhī Guñcā Tire....

jo bhī guñcā tire hoṇṭhoṃ pe khilā karatā hai
vo mirī taṅgī-e-dāmāṃ kā gilā karatā hai

dera se āja mirā sara hai tire zānū para
ye vo rutbā hai jo śāhoṃ ko milā karatā hai

maiṃ to baiṭhā hūm̐ dabāe hue tūfānoṃ ko
tū mire dila ke dhaḍ̂akane kā gilā karatā hai

rāta yūm̐ cām̐da ko dekhā hai nadī meṃ raqsāṃ
jaise jhūmara tire māthe pe hilā karatā hai

kauna kāfira tujhe ilazāma-e-tag̲h̲āfula degā
jo bhī karatā hai mohabbata kā gilā karatā hai

* * *

जो भी गुंचा तिरे.....

जो भी गुंचा[1] तिरे होंठों पे खिला करता है
वो मिरी तंगी-ए-दामां[2] का गिला करता है

देर से आज मिरा सर है तिरे ज़ानू पर
ये वो रुत्बा है जो शाहों को मिला करता है

मैं तो बैठा हूँ दबाए हुए तूफ़ानों को
तू मिरे दिल के धड़कने का गिला करता है

रात यूँ चाँद को देखा है नदी में रक़्सां[3]
जैसे झूमर तिरे माथे पे हिला करता है

कौन काफ़िर तुझे इलज़ाम-ए-तग़ाफ़ुल[4] देगा
जो भी करता है मोहब्बत का गिला करता है

* * *

1. कली 2. छोटा दामन 3. नाचते हुए 4. लापरवाही का आरोप

نہیں دھڑکا مجھے....

نہیں دھڑکا مجھے رسوائیوں کا
سفر درپیش ہے تنہائیوں کا

چھُپا بیٹھا ہوں اپنی خامشی میں
گیا موسم وہ بزم آرائیوں کا

یہیں بس جاؤں دل تو چاہتا ہے
مگر یہ شہر ہے ہر جائیوں کا

ذرا دیکھو مرے دل میں اُتر کر
سمندر نام ہے گہرائیوں کا

قتیلؔ آنکھوں میں ہے تصویرِ یوسف
کرم مجھ پر بھی ہے کچھ بھائیوں کا

* * *

I AM NOT AFRAID.....

I am not afraid that I will be disdained
The trek ahead of me may leave me deranged

I am now hiding within my solitariness
Gone are the days when I used to entertain

My heart wishes to settle in this habitat
But love around here is not well sustained

You may just dive in my heart and see
That it is ocean deep, fathoms unrestrained

Like Yousaf's fate at the hands of his siblings
O "Qateel", I also feel fated and ordained

* * *

Nahīṃ Dhaḍkā Mujhe...

nahīṃ dhaḍakā mujhe rusvāiyoṃ kā
safara dara peśa hai tanhāiyoṃ kā

chupā baiṭhā hūm̐ apanī khāmuśī meṃ
gayā mausama vo bazma ārāiyoṃ kā

yahīṃ basa jāuṃ dila to cāhatā hai
magara ye śahara hai harajāiyoṃ kā

zarā dekho mire dila meṃ utara kara
samandara nāma hai gaharāiyoṃ kā

"qatīla" āṃkhoṃ meṃ hai tasvīra-e-yūsufa
karama mujha para bhī hai kucha bhāiyoṃ kā

* * *

नहीं धड़का मुझे.....

नहीं धड़का मुझे रुसवाइयों का
सफ़र दर पेश है तन्हाइयों का

छुपा बैठा हूँ अपनी खामुशी में
गया मौसम वो बज़्म आराइयों[1] का

यहीं बस जाऊं दिल तो चाहता है
मगर ये शह्र है हरजाइयों का

ज़रा देखो मिरे दिल में उतर कर
समंदर नाम है गहराइयों का

"क़तील" आंखों में है तस्वीर-ए-यूसुफ़[2]
करम मुझ पर भी है कुछ भाईयों का

* * *

---

1. महफ़िल सजाना 2. प्रसिद्ध अवतार जो सौन्दर्य में अपनी मिसाल आप थे और इसी कारण उनके शेष भाईयों ने उनसे जलकर उन्हें कुएं में फेंक दिया था

راستے یاد نہیں راہنما....

راستے یاد نہیں راہنما یاد نہیں
اب مجھے کچھ تری گلیوں کے سوا یاد نہیں

ایک وعدہ تھا جو شیشے کی طرح ٹوٹ گیا
حادثہ کب یہ ہوا ، کیسے ہوا یاد نہیں

ہم دِیا کرتے تھے اغیار کو طعنہ جن کا
اب تو ہم کو بھی وہ آدابِ وفا یاد نہیں

وضع داری سے ہے مجبور مرا پیار قتیلؔ
سب پُرانے ہیں کوئی داغ نیا یاد نہیں

* * *

I SCARCE REMEMBER.....

I scarce remember who led all the way
Except your alley where I was led astray

Your promise was one that broke like brittle glass
How it all happened, I do not recollect the day

We used to taunt the rivals for their bad behaviour
We lover look our oversight, now in our affray

O "Qateel", I feel compelled by my own decorum
All my scars are old, new scars not to say

* * *

Rāste Yād Nahīṃ Rāhnumā....

rāste yāda nahīṃ rāhanumā yāda nahīṃ
aba mujhe kucha tirī galiyoṃ ke sivā yāda nahīṃ

eka vādā thā jo śīśe kī taraha ṭūṭa gayā
hādasā kaba ye huā, kaise huā, yāda nahīṃ!

hama diyā karate the aghiyāra ko tānā jinakā
aba to hamako bhī vo ādāba-e-vafā yāda nahīṃ

vazādārī se hai majabūra mirā pyāra "qatīla"
saba purāne haiṃ koī dāgha nayā yāda nahīṃ

✸ ✸ ✸

रास्ते याद नहीं राहनुमा.....

रास्ते याद नहीं राहनुमा[1] याद नहीं
अब मुझे कुछ तिरी गलियों के सिवा याद नहीं

एक वादा था जो शीशे की तरह टूट गया
हादसा[2] कब ये हुआ, कैसे हुआ, याद नहीं!

हम दिया करते थे अग़्यार[3] को ताना जिनका
अब तो हमको भी वो आदाब-ए-वफ़ा याद नहीं

वज़ादारी[4] से है मजबूर मिरा प्यार "क़तील"
सब पुराने हैं कोई दाग़ नया याद नहीं

* * *

---

1. रास्ता दिखाने वाला 2. दुर्घटना 3. ग़ैर, पराए 4. पासदारी

کوئی مقامِ سکوں....

کوئی مقامِ سکوں راستے میں آیا نہیں
ہزاروں پیڑ ہیں لیکن کہیں بھی سایا نہیں

بھٹک رہے ہیں ابھی تک مسافر انِ وصال
ترے جمال نے کوئی دِیا جلایا نہیں

بکھر گیا ہے خلا میں کرن کرن ہوکر
وہ چاند جو کسی پہلو میں جگمگایا نہیں

اُجڑ گیا تھا کسی زلزلے میں شہرِ وفا
نجانے پھر اُسے ہم نے بھی کیوں بَسایا نہیں

قتیؔل کیسے کٹے گی یہ دوپہر غم کی
مرے نصیب میں ان گیسوؤں کا سایا نہیں

* * *

ON OUR WAY.....

On our way, no resting places come our way
In spite of thousand trees, the sun was in sway

Those seeking, fulfilment are groping in the dark
Your incandescence could not dispel shades of gray

The moon that did not reflect resplendence all around
Will be scattered bit by bit and will decay

The citadel of fealty collapsed in a quake
To populate anew, why this delay

How, O "Qateel", I may survive this seperation
As I am so fated to suffer this dismay

* * *

Koī Maqām-E-Sakūṃ...

koī maqāma-e-sakūṃ rāste meṃ āyā nahīṃ
hazāra peḍa haiṃ lekina kahīṃ bhī sāyā nahīṃ

bhaṭaka rahe haiṃ abhī taka musāfirāna-e-visāla
tire jamāla ne koī diyā jalāyā nahīṃ

bikhara gayā hai khalā meṃ kirana-kirana hokara
vo cānda jo kisī pahalū meṃ jagamagāyā nahīṃ

ujaḍa gayā thā kisī zala-zale meṃ śahra-e-vafā
na jāne phira use hamane bhī kyoṃ basāyā nahīṃ

"qatīla" kaise kaṭegī ye dopahara ghama kī!
mire nasība meṃ una gesuoṃ kā sāyā nahīṃ

* * *

कोई मक़ाम-ए-सकूं....

कोई मक़ाम–ए–सकूं रास्ते में आया नहीं
हज़ार पेड़ हैं लेकिन कहीं भी साया नहीं

भटक रहे हैं अभी तक मुसाफ़िरान–ए–विसाल[1]
तिरे जमाल ने कोई दिया जलाया नहीं

बिखर गया है ख़ला[2] में किरन–किरन होकर
वो चांद जो किसी पहलू में जगमगाया नहीं

उजड़ गया था किसी ज़ल–ज़ले में शह्र–ए–वफ़ा
न जाने फिर उसे हमने भी क्यों बसाया नहीं

"क़तील" कैसे कटेगी ये दोपहर ग़म की!
मिरे नसीब में उन गेसुओं का साया नहीं

* * *

---

1. मिलन वाले यात्री 2. अनन्त

اک اک پتھر جوڑ کے....

اک اک پتھر جوڑ کے میں نے جو دیوار بنائی ہے
جھانکوں اس کے پیچھے تو رسوائی ہی رسوائی ہے

یوں لگتا ہے سوتے جاگتے اوروں کا محتاج ہوں میں
آنکھیں میری اپنی ہیں پر اُن میں نیند پرائی ہے

دیکھ رہے ہیں سب حیرت سے نیلے نیلے پانی کو
پوچھے کون سمندر سے تجھ میں کتنی گہرائی ہے

آج ہوا معلوم مجھے اس شہر کے چند سیانوں سے
اپنی راہ بدلتے رہنا سب سے بڑی دانائی ہے

توڑ گئے پیمانِ وفا اس دَور میں کیسے کیسے لوگ
یہ مت سوچ قتیلؔ کہ بس اک یار ترا ہرجائی ہے

* * *

BRICK BY BRICK.....

Brick by brick this edifice of love I have built
If I peep beyond, I suffer sense of guilt

Asleep or wide awake, I feel beholden to others
Sleep that in my eyes I hold, is not inbuilt

All see the blue water with a sense of awe
They don't quite appreciate ocean has its silt

I came to know to day from wise folk
The greatest wisdom lies in ever changing your tilt

How many people in this era have change their fidelity
Don't ever think, O "Qateel", your beloved is upto hilt

* * *

Ik-Ik Patthar Joḍ Ke....

ika-ika patthara joḍa ke mainne jo dīvāra banāī hai
jhāṅkūṃ usake pīche to rusvāī hī rusvāī hai

yūṁ lagatā hai sote-jāgate auroṃ kā mohatāja hūṁ maiṃ
āṃkheṃ merī apanī haiṃ para unameṃ nīnda parāī hai

dekha rahe haiṃ saba hairata se nīle-nīle pānī ko!
pūche kauna samandara se tujha meṃ kitanī gaharāī hai

āja huā mālūma mujhe isa śahra ke canda siyānoṃ se
apanī rāha badalate rahanā sabase baḍī dānāī hai

toḍa gae paimāna-e-vafā isa daura meṃ kaise-kaise loga
yaha mata soca "qatīla" ki basa ika yāra tirā harajāī hai

✸ ✸ ✸

इक-इक पत्थर जोड़ के.....

इक–इक पत्थर जोड़ के मैंने जो दीवार बनाई है
झांकूं उसके पीछे तो रुस्वाई ही रुस्वाई है

यूँ लगता है सोते–जागते औरों का मोहताज हूँ मैं
आंखें मेरी अपनी हैं पर उनमें नींद पराई है

देख रहे हैं सब हैरत से नीले–नीले पानी को!
पूछे कौन समन्दर से तुझ में कितनी गहराई है

आज हुआ मालूम मुझे इस शह्र के चंद सियानों से
अपनी राह बदलते रहना सबसे बड़ी दानाई[1] है

तोड़ गए पैमान–ए–वफ़ा इस दौर में कैसे–कैसे लोग
यह मत सोच "क़तील" कि बस इक यार तिरा हरजोई है

* * *

1. चतुराई

وفا کے شیش محل....

وفا کے شیش محل میں سجالیا میں نے
وہ ایک دل جسے پتّھر بنالیا میں نے

یہ سوچ کر کہ نہ ہو تاک میں خوشی کوئی
غموں کی اوٹ میں خود کو چھُپا لیا میں نے

کبھی نہ ختم کیا میں نے روشنی کا محاذ
اگر چراغ بجھا، دل جَلا لیا میں نے

کمال یہ ہے کہ دشمن پہ جو چلانا تھا
وہ تِیر اپنے کلیجے پہ کھالیا میں نے

قتیلؔ جِس کی عَداوَت میں ایک پیار بھی تھا
اُس آدمی کو گلے سے لگالیا میں نے

* * *

ON A HIGH PEDESTAL.....

On a high pedestal I placed my fidelity
I made a heart an icon with all sincerity

My joys not to be overtaken by my sorrows
Overwrought I thought, I should conceal my identity

I never accepted defeat at the hands of the darkness
If candle was extinguished, I lit my heart with alacrity

The dart which was meant to target the rival
I accepted the same dart with utmost vulnerability

A person who showed amity along with animosity
I embraced the same parson, O "Qateel", with reciprocity

* * *

Vafā Ke Śīś Mahal..

vafā ke śīśa mahala meṃ sajā liyā mainne
vo eka dila jise patthara banā liyā mainne

ye socakara ki na ho tāka meṃ k͟husī koī
g͟hamoṃ kī oṭa meṃ k͟huda ko chipā liyā mainne

kabhī na k͟hatma kiyā mainne rauśanī kā muhāza
agara cirāg͟ha bujhā, dila jalā liyā mainne

kamāla yaha hai ki duśmana pe jo calānā
vo tīra apane kaleje pe khā liyā mainne

"qatīla" jisakā adāvata meṃ eka pyāra bhī thā
usa ādamī ko gale se lagā liyā mainne

* * *

वफ़ा के शीश महल.....

वफ़ा के शीश महल में सजा लिया मैंने
वो एक दिल जिसे पत्थर बना लिया मैंने

ये सोचकर कि न हो ताक में ख़ुशी कोई
ग़मों की ओट में ख़ुद को छिपा लिया मैंने

कभी न ख़त्म किया मैंने रौशनी का मुहाज़[1]
अगर चिराग़ बुझा, दिल जला लिया मैंने

कमाल यह है कि दुश्मन पे जो चलाना था
वो तीर अपने कलेजे पे खा लिया मैंने

"क़तील" जिसका अदावत[2] में एक प्यार भी था
उस आदमी को गले से लगा लिया मैंने

* * *

---

1. मोर्चा 2. दुश्मनी

یار کیوں گُریزاں ہے....

یار کیوں گُریزاں ہے، سیدھی راہ چلنے سے
منزلیں نہیں ملتیں، راستے بدلنے سے

جو بھی رنگ ہے تیرا، بس وہی غنیمت ہے
چہرے کب نِکھرتے ہیں، منہ پہ خاک ملنے سے

تیز دھوپ میں آئی، ایسی لہر سردی کی
موم کا ہر اک پُتلا بچ گیا پگھلنے سے

آپ اپنے جرموں کا، بن گئے ثبوت آخر
ہاتھ جو معطّر تھے، پھول کو مَسلنے سے

سو کے تُو گنوا بیٹھا، رَت جگوں کی رعنائی
اب قتیلؔ کیا حاصل تیرے ہاتھ ملنے سے

* * *

TO TREAD THE RIGHTEOUS...

To tread the righteous path, why beloved hesitates
One cannot find destination, if one dithers and dilates

We accept your coloration with a sense of resignation
How can a face shine, if dust militates

In the scorching sun, a cold wave has entered
Every wax effigy was saved by sun's dictates

You provided your own proof of your complicity
By your crushing of the flowers, scent from hand permeates

You all but lost the romance of your nocturnal vigil
What use, O "Qateel" now, if one ruminates

* * *

Yār Kyoṃ Gurezāṃ Hai....

yāra kyoṃ gurezāṃ hai, sīdhī rāha calane se
mañzileṃ nahīṃ milatīṃ rāste badalane se

jo bhī raṅga hai terā basa vahī g̲h̲anīmata hai
cehare kaba nikharate haiṃ, mum̐ha pe k̲h̲āka malane se

teza dhūpa meṃ āī aisī lahara sardī kī
moma kā hara ika putalā, baca gayā pighalane se

āpa apane jurmoṃ kā bana gae sabūta āk̲h̲ira
hātha jo moattira the, phūla ko masalane se

so ke tū gam̐vā baiṭhā, rata jagoṃ kī rānāī
aba "qatīla" kyā hāsila tere hātha malane se

* * *

यार क्यों गुरेज़ां है.....

यार क्यों गुरेज़ां[1] है, सीधी राह चलने से
मंज़िलें नहीं मिलतीं रास्ते बदलने से

जो भी रंग है तेरा बस वही ग़नीमत है
चेहरे कब निखरते हैं, मुँह पे ख़ाक मलने से

तेज़ धूप में आई ऐसी लहर सर्दी की
मोम का हर इक पुतला, बच गया पिघलने से

आप अपने जुर्मों का बन गए सबूत आख़िर
हाथ जो मोअत्तिर[2] थे, फूल को मसलने से

सो के तू गँवा बैठा, रत जगों की रानाई[3]
अब "क़तील" क्या हासिल तेरे हाथ मलने से

* * *

---

1. हिचकिचाहट 2. सुगंधित 3. सुंदरता

بظاہر بزمِ آرائی....

بظاہر بزم آرائی بہت ہے
بھرے شہروں میں تنہائی بہت ہے

نہایت خوبصورت ہے یہ دُنیا
مگر ہنگامہ آرائی بہت ہے

پرانے جوہڑوں کا ہے یہ عالم
کہ پانی کم ہے اور کائی بہت ہے

محبّت کی کہانی منفرد تھی
مگر دنیا نے دہرائی بہت ہے

قتیلؔ اَب کچھ دنوں سے قاتلوں میں
ہماری بھی پذیرائی بہت ہے

* * *

APPARENTLY ENCLAVES.....

Apparently enclaves are populated
Crowded habitats, however, are isolated

The world, no doubt, is well embellished
With animosity, however, it is animated

Old water holes are in a sorry state
Silt abounds, water has evaporated

Unique as the tale of love was
But it has bee overstated

Lately, O "Qateel", among the detractors
Happily, we are not berated

• ✸ ✸ ✸

Bazāhir Bazm-Ārāī....

bazāhira bazma-ārāī bahuta hai
bhare śaharoṃ meṃ tanhāī bahuta hai

nihāyata <u>kh</u>ūba sūrata hai ye duniyā
magara haṅgāmā ārāī bahuta hai

purāne johaḋoṃ kā hai ye ālama
ki pānī kama hai aura kāī bahuta hai

mohabbata kī kahānī munfarida thī
magara duniyā ne doharāī bahuta hai

"qatīla" aba kucha dinoṃ se qātiloṃ meṃ
hamārī bhī pazīrāī bahuta hai

* * *

बज़ाहिर बज़्म-आराई.....

बज़ाहिर[1] बज़्म–आराई[2] बहुत है
भरे शहरों में तन्हाई बहुत है

निहायत खूब सूरत है ये दुनिया
मगर हंगामा आराई बहुत है

पुराने जोहड़ों का है ये आलम
कि पानी कम है और काई बहुत है

मोहब्बत की कहानी मुन्फ़रिद[3] थी
मगर दुनिया ने दोहराई बहुत है

"क़तील" अब कुछ दिनों से क़ातिलों में
हमारी भी पज़ीराई[4] बहुत है

* * *

1. प्रकट में 2. रौनक़, महफ़िल सजाना 3. सबसे अलग
4. पहुँच

جب بھی دریا بارشوں کے....

جب بھی دریا بارشوں کے پانیوں سے بھر گئے
تیَر نے ہم بھی بدن سے باندھ کر پتھر گئے

تک رہی تھی راستہ صرف اک گھڑی دیوار کی
دیر سے ہم لوٹ کر جس رات اپنے گھر گئے

دل کی سرکوبی کو نکلے آرزوؤں کے ہجوم
ایک دشمن کے تعاقب میں کئی لشکر گئے

مجرموں کی پردہ پوشی سے بڑا کیا جُرم ہے
وہ بھی کم ظالم نہ تھے جو ظالموں سے ڈر گئے

اُف جوانی کے وہ آوارہ سے کچھ لمحے قتیلؔ
آپ بھی رُسوا ہوئے ہم کو بھی رسوا کر گئے

* * *

WHENEVER.....

Whenever rivers swollen by rains were in spate
To remain afloat, round our waist, we tied some weight

Wall on the clock was chiding upon our return
When from nocturnal jaunt, we came home so late

Longings, layer upon layer, tried to cure our heart
So many to put one knotted ring straight

To cover a crime is no less than the basic crime
Those who tried to intimidate and to perpetuate

O "Qateel", they were moments of youthful exuberence
To defame and to shame, enough to implicate

* * *

Jab Bhī Dariyā Bāriśoṃ Ke....

jaba bhī dariyā bāriśoṃ ke pāniyoṃ se bhara gae
tairane hama bhī badana se bāndha kara patthara gae

taka rahī thī rāstā sirfa ika ghaḋī dīvāra kī
dera se hama lauṭa kara jisa rāta apane ghara gae

dila kī sarakobī ko nikale ārazuoṃ ke hujūma
eka duśmana ke taāqquba meṃ kaī laśkara gae

mujarimoṃ kī pardā pośī se baḋā kyā jurma hai
vo bhī kama zālima na the jo zālimoṃ se ḍara gae

ufa javānī ke vo āvārā se kucha lamhe "qatīla"
āpa bhī rusvā hue hama ko bhī rusvā kara gae

* * *

जब भी दरिया बारिशों के.....

जब भी दरिया बारिशों के पानियों से भर गए
तैरने हम भी बदन से बांध कर पत्थर गए

तक रही थी रास्ता सिर्फ़ इक घड़ी दीवार की
देर से हम लौट कर जिस रात अपने घर गए

दिल की सरकोबी[1] को निकले आरज़ुओं के हुजूम
एक दुश्मन के तआक़्क़ुब[2] में कई लश्कर[3] गए

मुजरिमों की पर्दा पोशी[4] से बड़ा क्या जुर्म है
वो भी कम ज़ालिम न थे जो ज़ालिमों से डर गए

उफ़ जवानी के वो आवारा से कुछ लम्हे "क़तील"
आप भी रुस्वा हुए हम को भी रुस्वा कर गए

* * *

1. कुचलना 2. पीछा 3. सेना 4. छिपाना

مہربانی سے اگر پیش....

مہربانی سے اگر پیش بھی آئے کچھ لوگ
دھوپ میں لپٹے ہوئے دے گئے سائے کچھ لوگ

میں نے آواز اٹھائی تھی رواجوں کے خلاف
برچھیاں لے کے گھروں سے نکل آئے کچھ لوگ

جب وہ بچ نکلے تو پانی میں مجھے پھینک دیا
کود کر میں نے جو دریا میں بچائے کچھ لوگ

کام کے لوگ وطن میں بھی نہیں تھے کمیاب
پھر بھی کچھ لوگوں نے باہر سے منگائے کچھ لوگ

بارہا میں نے جوانی کے چوراہے میں قتیلؔ
پی کے اپنا ہی لہو، جھومتے پائے کچھ لوگ

* * *

EVEN IF SOME PEOPLE.....

Even if some people treated us with kindness
Even then some people had treated us with harshness

I had raised my voice against entrenched tradition
People had retaliated with an utmost viciousness

The people I had saved from drowning in the river
They tossed me in the river in their thankfulness

There was no shortage of people with useful hands
Even then some people had imported hands for usefulness

Many a time, I, O "Qateel" found oddly enough
People had shot themselves in foot, in their youthfulness

* * *

Meharbānī Se Agar Peś....

meharabānī se agara peśa bhī āe kucha loga
dhūpa meṃ lipaṭe hue de gae sāe kucha loga

mainne āvāza uṭhāī thī rivājoṃ ke khilāfa
barchiyāṃ lekara gharoṃ se nikala āe kucha loga

jaba vo baca nikale to pānī meṃ mujhe pheṅka diyā
kūda kara mainne jo dariyā meṃ bacāe kucha loga

kāma ke loga vatana meṃ bhī nahīṃ athe kamayāba
phira bhī kucha logoṃ ne bāhara se maṅgāe kuda loga

bārahā mainne javānī ke dorāhe pe "qatīla"
pīke apanā hī lahū jhūmate pāe kucha loga

* * *

मेहरबानी से अगर पेश.....

मेहरबानी से अगर पेश भी आए कुछ लोग
धूप में लिपटे हुए दे गए साए कुछ लोग

मैंने आवाज़ उठाई थी रिवाजों के ख़िलाफ़
बर्छियां लेकर घरों से निकल आए कुछ लोग

जब वो बच निकले तो पानी में मुझे फेंक दिया
कूद कर मैंने जो दरिया में बचाए कुछ लोग

काम के लोग वतन में भी नहीं थे कमयाब[1]
फिर भी कुछ लोगों ने बाहर से मंगाए कुछ लोग

बारहा मैंने जवानी के दोराहे पे "क़तील"
पीके अपना ही लहू झूमते पाए कुछ लोग

* * *

---

1. कम संख्या में 2. रक्त

ہر شے سے بیگانہ اچھا

ہر شے سے بیگانہ اچھا
لوگو! میں دیوانہ اچھا

ہم سب پر جو بیت چکی ہے
اُس کا بھول ہی جانا اچھا

نعروں کے اس شور میں بھائی
شہروں سے ویرانہ اچھا

جس ماحول میں ہم زندہ ہیں
اِس سے تو مرجانا اچھا

یارِ قتیلؔ نئے لوگوں سے
ایک ہی یار پُرانا اچھا

٭ ٭ ٭

'TIS GOOD.....

'Tis good I couldn't care less
'Tis good, I am mad nevertheless

What we all have gone through
'Tis good to remember less and less

In the noisy rhetoric, O friend
Better desert's solitariness

In the environ we live and breathe
Swan song is better than caress

"Qateel", O friend take it from me
Better than new acquaintance, old friendliness

* * *

Har Śay Se Begānā Acchā....

hara śaya se begānā acchā
logoṃ! maiṃ dīvānā acchā

hama saba para jo bīta cukī hai
usakā bhūla hī jānā acchā

nāroṃ ke isa śora meṃ bhāī
śahroṃ se vīrānā acchā

jisa māhaula meṃ hama zindā haiṃ
isa se to mara jānā acchā

yāra "qatīla" nae logoṃ se
eka hī yāra purānā acchājña

* * *

हर शय से बेगाना अच्छा.....

हर शय[1] से बेगाना अच्छा
लोगों! मैं दीवाना अच्छा

हम सब पर जो बीत चुकी है
उसका भूल ही जाना अच्छा

नारों के इस शोर में भाई
शहरों से वीराना अच्छा

जिस माहौल में हम ज़िंदा हैं
इस से तो मर जाना अच्छा

यार "क़तील" नए लोगों से
एक ही यार पुराना अच्छा

* * *

1. वस्तु

دو چہرگی

وہ سب کے دل میں بس بن کے اعتبار وفا
یہ ایک خاص ادا بے مثال ہے اس کی
نظر کسی کی طرف اور دل کسی کے ساتھ
عجب سیاستِ حسن و جمال ہے اس کی

* * *

کربِ انا

اُس کی حسین راتوں کا جو لے سکے حساب
کہتی ہے وہ ابھی کوئی پیدا نہیں ہوا
یا اُس نے دل کسی کو دیا ہی نہیں ابھی
یا اُس پہ آج تک کوئی شیدا نہیں ہوا

* * *

DOUBLE FACE

Beloved should win every heart with fealty
This is a unique strategem, beloved's own speciality
Seeing in one direction, loving someone else
Strange are the ways of beloved's bounden beauty

* * *

EGO'S PAIN

Who can keep a count of beloved's cozy nights
beloved thinks no one yet has been born
Either beloved has never given own heart
Or any one to love has not yet been born

* * *

Do Cehargī....

vo sabake dila meṃ base banake etabāra-e-vafā
ye eka khāsa adā be misāla hai usakī
nazara kisī kī tarafa aura dila kisī ke sātha
ajaba riyāsata-e-husna-o-jamāla hai usakī

* * *

Karb-E-Anā....

usakī hasīna rātoṃ kā jo le sake hisāba
kahatī hai vo abhī koī paidā nahīṃ huā
yā usane dila kisī ko diyā hī nahīṃ abhī
yā usape āja taka koī śaidā nahīṃ huā

* * *

दो चेहरगी[1]

वो सबके दिल में बसे बनके एतबार–ए–वफ़ा
ये एक ख़ास अदा बे मिसाल है उसकी
नज़र किसी की तरफ़ और दिल किसी के साथ
अजब रियासत–ए–हुस्न–ओ–जमाल[2] है उसकी

✹ ✹ ✹

कर्ब-ए-अना[3]

उसकी हसीन रातों का जो ले सके हिसाब
कहती है वो अभी कोई पैदा नहीं हुआ
या उसने दिल किसी को दिया ही नहीं अभी
या उसपे आज तक कोई शैदा[4] नहीं हुआ

✹ ✹ ✹

1. दोहरा रूप 2. हसीनों की राजनीति 3. अहंम का दर्द
4. आशिक़

تحقیق

سمٹ سکا نہ کبھی زندگی کا پھیلاؤ
کہیں بھی ختم غمِ عاشقی نہیں ہوتا
نکل ہی آتی ہے کوئی نہ کوئی گنجائش
کسی کا پیار کبھی آخری نہیں ہوتا

* * *

دلاسہ

یقیناً یہ انوکھا حادثہ ہے
کہ ہم ملتے ہی پھر سے بٹ گئے ہیں
کسک سی رہ گئی ہے دل میں لیکن
چلو کچھ دن تو اچھے کٹ گئے ہیں

* * *

RESEARCH

The circle of life cannot be circumscribed
Woes of love can never be fully described
Somehow somewhere there is this loophole
Anyone's love a final cannot be prescribed

* * *

CONSOLATION

Surely this is a strange circumstance
That soon after meeting we are separated
There is this lingering feeling in the heart
That at least for few days we have been elated

* * *

Tahqīq....

simaṭa sakā na kabhī zindagī kā phailāva
kahīṃ bhī khatma ghama-e-āśiqī nahīṃ hotā
nikala hī ātī hai koī na koī guñjāiśa
kisī kā pyāra kabhī ākhirī nahīṃ hotā

* * *

Dilāsā....

yaqīnana ye anokhā hādasā hai
ki hama milate hī phira se baṭa gae haiṃ
kasaka sī raha gaī hai dila meṃ lekina
calo kucha dina to acche kaṭa gae haiṃ

* * *

तहक़ीक़[1]

सिमट सका न कभी ज़िंदगी का फैलाव
कहीं भी ख़त्म ग़म-ए-आशिक़ी नहीं होता
निकल ही आती है कोई न कोई गुंजाइश
किसी का प्यार कभी आख़िरी नहीं होता

* * *

दिलासा

यक़ीनन ये अनोखा हादसा[2] है
कि हम मिलते ही फिर से बट गए हैं
कसक सी रह गई है दिल में लेकिन
चलो कुछ दिन तो अच्छे कट गए हैं

* * *

---

1. खोज 2. दुर्घटना

تارکین

حاصل رہا ہو جو ترکِ سکونت سے پیشتر
سب نے وہ امتیاز بھی اپنا گنوالیا
لالچ میں ہرنیاں کسی دریا میں جا بسیں
اور مچھلیوں نے دشت کو مسکن بنالیا

٭ ٭ ٭

کیریکٹر

اس سے بچھڑے ہوئے گو ایک زمانہ بیتا
لیکن اس بات سے تکلیف مجھے ہوتی ہے
کر گئی جس کے لئے ترکِ تعلق مجھ سے
پالیا اس کو تو اب میرے لئے روتی ہے

٭ ٭ ٭

EMIGRANTS

What privilege they enjoyed before emigration
They all but lost that fair distinction
As if the forest deer dive into the river
And fish go to forest to go into extinction

* * *

CHARACTER

Though long from beloved I have been separated
With the one aspect I am overwrought
The person for whom beloved broke with me
Found at last, but longs for me a lot

* * *

Tārkīn....

hāsila rahā jo tarka-e-sakūnata se peśtara
saba ne vo imtiyāza bhī apanā gam̐vā diyā
lālaca meṃ hiraniyāṃ kisī dariyā meṃ jā basīṃ
aura machaliyoṃ ne daśta meṃ maskana banā liyā

* * *

Kairekṭar....

usase bichaḍe hue go eka zamānā bītā
lekina isa bāta se taklīfa mujhe hotī hai
kara gaī jisa ke lie tarka-e-taalluqa mujha se
pāliyā usako to aba mere lie rotī hai

* * *

तारकीन[1]

हासिल रहा जो तर्क-ए-सकूनत[2] से पेश्तर
सब ने वो इम्तियाज़[3] भी अपना गँवा दिया
लालच में हिरनियां किसी दरिया में जा बसीं
और मछलियों ने दश्त[4] में मस्कन[5] बना लिया

✹ ✹ ✹

कैरेक्टर

उससे बिछड़े हुए गो एक ज़माना बीता
लेकिन इस बात से तक्लीफ़ मुझे होती है
कर गई जिस के लिए तर्क-ए-तअल्लुक़[6] मुझ से
पालिया उसको तो अब मेरे लिए रोती है

✹ ✹ ✹

---

1. पलायन करने वाले प्रवासी 2. प्रवास छोड़ने से पहले
3. विशेषता 4. जंगल 5. आवास 6. सम्बंध विच्छेद

خیر اگر چاہتے ہو....

خیر اگر چاہتے ہو سَروں کی
راہ لو اپنے اپنے گھروں کی

نفرتیں بونے والوں کو مژدہ
فصل تیار ہے خنجروں کی

نیک بندوں کے ہاتھ آگئے ہیں
قسمتیں جاگ اٹھیں پتھروں کی

اہلِ ایماں ہیں دست و گریباں
اب ضرورت نہیں کافروں کی

اس نے کھوئی قتیلؔ اپنی منزل
پیروی جس نے کی رہبروں کی

* * *

IF YOU WANT SAFETY.....

If you want safety of your head
Then keep within the safety of your homestead

Harvest of fire and sword is ready
Glad tidings for those sowing hatred

Well intentioned folk have found excess
For rock and stone as their kindred

Infidels are not needed any more
With men of faith in fighting instead

O "Qateel", he surely went astray
Who by rogues let himself be led

* * *

Khair Agar Cāhate Ho....

khera agara cāhate ho saroṃ kī
rāha lo apane apane gharoṃ kī

nafarateṃ bone vāloṃ ko muzdā
fasala taiyāra hai khañjaroṃ kī

neka bandoṃ ke hātha ā gae haiṃ
qismateṃ jāga uṭhīṃ pattharoṃ kī

ahla-e-īmāṃ haiṃ dasta-o-girebāṃ
aba zarūrata nahīṃ kāfiroṃ kī

usane khoī "qatīla" apanī mañzila
pairavī jisane kī rahabāroṃ kī

* * *

ख़ैर अगर चाहते हो.....

ख़ैर अगर चाहते हो सरों की
राह लो अपने अपने घरों की

नफ़रतें बोने वालों को मुज़्दा[1]
फ़सल तैयार है ख़ंजरों की

नेक बंदों[2] के हाथ आ गए हैं
क़िस्मतें जाग उठीं पत्थरों की

अह्ल–ए–ईमां हैं दस्त–ओ–गिरेबाँ[3]
अब ज़रूरत नहीं काफ़िरों की

उसने खोई "क़तील" अपनी मंज़िल
पैरवी[4] जिसने की रहबरों[5] की

* * *

---

1. शुभ समाचार 2. भले इंसान 3. आपस में लड़ना
4. अनुसरण 5. रास्ता दिखाने वाले

رَچی ہے رَت جگوں....

رچی ہے رَت جگوں کی چاندنی جن کی جبینوں میں
قتیلؔ اک عمر گزری ہے ہماری ان حسینوں میں

وہ جن کے آنچلوں سے زندگی تخلیق ہوتی ہے
دھڑکتا ہے ہمارا دل ابھی تک اُن کے سینوں میں

زمانہ پارسائی کی حدوں تک ہم کو لے آیا
مگر ہم آج بھی رسوا ہیں اپنے ہم نشینوں میں

تلاش اُن کو ہماری تو نہیں پوچھو ذرا اُن سے
وہ قاتل جو لیے پھرتے ہیں خنجر آستینوں میں

سکونت بار جب بن جائے بُنیادِ رفاقت پر
مکاں تقسیم ہو جاتے ہیں خود اپنے مکینوں میں

* * *

THOSE WHO SHOW.....

Those who show sleeplessness on their resplendent forehead
O "Qateel", we have spent our life among those beloved

Whose very raiment gives sustenence to life
Our heart beat is shared in their bosoms kindred

The circumstances have brought us to the ways of piety
But even today we are treated by our peers with dread

Just ask them if they are searching around for us
Those detractors who are after our very blood

When ownership becomes the basis of our amity
Then homes become divided on the basis of hatred

* * *

Racī Hai Ratjagoṃ....

racī hai ratajagoṃ kī cāṁdanī jinakī jabīnoṃ meṃ
"qatīla" ika umra guzarī hai hamārī una hasīnoṃ meṃ

vo jinake āṁcaloṃ se zindagī takhalīqa hotī hai
dhaḍ̂akatā hai hamārā dila aabhī taka unake sīnoṃ meṃ

zamānā pārasāī kī hadoṃ taka hamako le āyā
magara hama āja taka rusvā haiṃ apane hama naśīnoṃ meṃ

talāśa unako hamārī to nahīṃ pūcho zarā unase
vo qātila jo lie phirate haiṃ khañjara āstīnoṃ meṃ

sakūnata bāra jaba bana jāe buniyāda-e-rifāqata para
makāṃ taqsīma ho jāte haiṃ khuda apane makīnoṃ meṃ

* * *

रची है रतजगों.....

रची है रतजगों की चाँदनी जिनकी जबीनों[1] में
"क़तील" इक उम्र गुज़री है हमारी उन हसीनों में

वो जिनके आँचलों से ज़िंदगी तख़लीक़[2] होती है
धड़कता है हमारा दिल अभी तक उनके सीनों में

ज़माना पारसाई[3] की हदों तक हमको ले आया
मगर हम आज तक रुस्वा हैं अपने हम नशीनों में

तलाश उनको हमारी तो नहीं पूछो ज़रा उनसे
वो क़ातिल जो लिए फिरते हैं ख़ंजर आस्तीनों में

सकूनत[4] बार जब बन जाए बुनियाद–ए–रिफ़ाक़त[5] पर
मकां तक़्सीम हो जाते हैं ख़ुद अपने मकीनों[6] में

* * *

---

1. माथा 2. पैदा 3. भलाई 4. रहना 5. मेल–जोल की बिना
6. रहने वाले

دل والوں کی بات....

دل والوں کی بات چلی ہے افسانہ در افسانہ
میرے ساتھ کے جاگنے والو، تم نہ کہیں اب سو جانہ

پیار تو کرتی ہے سب دُنیا بات فقط ایثار کی ہے
محفل کو اس سے کیا مطلب شمع جلے یا پروانہ

میری خوشیاں بھی اَن دیکھی میرے غم بھی اَن دیکھے
جنگل کے پھولوں کا یارو کیا کِھلنا، کیا مرجھانا

پھولوں کی مانند کِھلے تھے ماضی میں دو پیار مرے
آج تلک منسوب ہے مجھ سے اک بانو اک سُلطانہ

کیوں غیروں سے پوچھ رہے ہو پتہ قتیلؔ شفائی کا
ایسا بھی گمنام نہیں ہے وہ شاعر، وہ دیوانہ

* * *

PEOPLE OF HEART.....

People of heart now the subject of discussion
Of people awake with me, don't go to sleep in depression

Though the whole world is in love, it is self denial that matters
For enclave it hardly matters, if candle or moth is in extinction

My happiness is unknown, my woes are unnoticed
It matters not if wild flowers wither in desolation

Like flowers, my love in the past has blossomed twice
Though anonymous till today, I am linked in succession

Why ask alien folk about "Qateel" Shifai
He is not so unknown, with his poetic obsession

* * *

Dil Vāloṃ Kī Bāt....

dila vāloṃ kī bāta calī hai afasānā dara afasānā
mere sātha ke jāgane vālo, tuma na kahīṃ aba so jānā

pyāra to karatī hai saba duniyā bāta faqata īsāra kī hai
mahafila ko isa se kyā matalaba, śammā jale yā paravānā

merī k͟husiyāṃ bhī ana dekhī, mere g͟hama bhī ana dekhe
jaṅgala ke phūloṃ kā yāro kyā khilanā kyā murjhānā

phūloṃ kī māninda khile the māzī meṃ do pyāra mire
āja talaka maṃsūba hai mujhase ika bāno ika sultānā

kyoṃ g͟hairoṃ se pūcha rahe ho patā "qatīla" śifāī kā
aisā bhī mumanāma nahīṃ he vo śāira vo dīvānā

* * *

दिल वालों की बात.....

दिल वालों की बात चली है अफ़साना दर अफ़साना
मेरे साथ के जागने वालो, तुम न कहीं अब सो जाना

प्यार तो करती है सब दुनिया बात फ़क़त ईसार[1] की है
महफ़िल को इस से क्या मतलब, शम्मा जले या परवाना

मेरी खुशियां भी अन देखी, मेरे ग़म भी अन देखे
जंगल के फूलों का यारो क्या खिलना क्या मुर्झाना

फूलों की मानिंद खिले थे माज़ी में दो प्यार मिरे
आज तलक मंसूब[2] है मुझसे इक बानो इक सुल्ताना

क्यों ग़ैरों से पूछ रहे हो पता "क़तील" शिफ़ाई का
ऐसा भी गुमनाम नहीं है वो शायर वो दीवाना

* * *

---

1. त्याग 2. जुड़ी हुई

بے وفاؤں میں تو نام....

بے وفاؤں میں تو نام اُس کا کہیں آتا نہیں
پھیر لے گا ہم سے وہ آنکھیں، یقیں آتا نہیں

اے ہواؤ! جاؤ اب تم ہی منالاؤ اسے
میرے کہنے سے تو وہ ناز آفریں آتا نہیں

پیار اس سے کیجئے صدیوں کی عمریں مانگ کر
بار بار ایسا زمانے میں حسیں آتا نہیں

اے سکوں روٹھا ہے کیوں میرے ہی دِل کے شہر سے
ہر کہیں جاتا ہے ظالم تو یہیں آتا نہیں

تہمتیں ساری اُسی کے دم سے تھیں ہم پر قتیلؔ
اب ہمارے پاس کوئی نکتہ چیں آتا نہیں

* * *

BELOVED'S NAME.....

Beloved's name is not among people without fealty
That we will not be betrayed, we can say with surety

O wafting wind, go and persuade beloved
As at my behest, that self-willed will not take pity

You long for beloved with long life to spare
As beautiful persons as beloved do not come with felicity

O peace of mind, why have you deserted me so
Beloved goes everywhere but not in my vicinity

All motives were attributed by our beloved, O "Qateel"
Now no detractor ever fixes fault with our proclivity

* * *

Be Vafāoṃ Meṃ To Nām....

be vafāoṃ meṃ to nāma usakā kahīṃ ātā nahīṃ
phera legā hama se vo āṃkheṃ, yaqīṃ ātā nahīṃ

ai havāoṃ! jāo aba tuma hī manā lāo use
mere kahane se to vo nāza āfarīṃ ātā nahīṃ

pyāra usase kījie sadiyoṃ kī umareṃ māṅga kara
bāra-bāra aisā zamānoṃ meṃ hasīṃ ātā nahīṃ

ai sakūṁ rūṭhā hai kyoṃ mere hī dila ke śahra se
hara kahīṃ jātā hai zālima tū yahīṃ ātā nahīṃ

tohmateṃ sārī usī ke dama se thīṃ hama para "qatīla"
aba hamāre pāsa koī nuqtācīṃ ātā nahīṃ

* * *

बे वफ़ाओं में तो नाम.....

बे वफ़ाओं में तो नाम उसका कहीं आता नहीं
फेर लेगा हम से वो आंखें, यक़ीं आता नहीं

ऐ हवाओं! जाओ अब तुम ही मना लाओ उसे
मेरे कहने से तो वो नाज़ आफ़रीं[1] आता नहीं

प्यार उससे कीजिए सदियों की उमरें मांग कर
बार–बार ऐसा ज़मानो में हसीं आता नहीं

ऐ सकूँ रूठा है क्यों मेरे ही दिल के शहर से
हर कहीं जाता है ज़ालिम तू यहीं आता नहीं

तोहमतें[2] सारी उसी के दम से थीं हम पर "क़तील"
अब हमारे पास कोई नुक्ताचीं[3] आता नहीं

* * *

---

1. नाज़ो–अंदाज़ वाला, नख़रे बाज़ 2. आरोप 3. टोकने वाला

میری آنکھوں میں....

میری آنکھوں میں کبھی پیار سے جھانکا بھی نہیں
وہ جفاکار کہ جھوٹا جو زباں کا بھی نہیں

جانے کیا سوچ کے دل دیتی ہے دنیا اُس کو؟
دیکھنے میں تو وہ ایسا کوئی بانکا بھی نہیں

دل دُکھانے کو نہ جانے وہ کدھر سے آیا؟
رہنے والا وہ محبت کے جہاں کا بھی نہیں

میں نے دیکھا نہیں اب تک کسی موسم کو ثبات
غم بہاروں کا نہیں ہے تو خزاں کا بھی نہیں

کیوں بھرے آہ کوئی دیکھ کے ٹوٹے دل کو
مقبرہ یہ تو کسی نور جہاں کا بھی نہیں

* * *

BELOVED HAS NEVER......

Beloved has never peeped into my eyes
That relenless person, even as a exercise

Why the whole world enamoured of that person
Who is not beautiful even in disguise

Where from that person came to cause misery
Surely not a resident of world of love precise

I have never seen constancy in any season
Woes don't belong to spring or autumn guise

This is no mausoleum of empress Noor Jehan
Why any one may raise any hues or cries

* * *

Merī Āṃkhoṃ Meṃ....

merī āṃkhoṃ meṃ kabhī pyāra se jhāṅkā bhī nahīṃ
vo jafākāra ki jhūṭhā jo zubāṃ kā bhī nahīṃ

jāne kyā soca ke dila detī hai duniyā usako
dekhane meṃ to vo aisā koī bāṅkā bhī nahīṃ

dila dukhāne ko na jāne vo kidhara se āyā?
rahane vālā vo mohabbata ke jahāṃ kā bhī nahīṃ

mainne dekhā nahīṃ aba taka kisī mausama ko sabāta
g͟hama bahāroṃ kā nahīṃ hai to k͟hizāṃ kā bhī nahīṃ

kyoṃ bhare āha koī dekha ke ṭūṭe dila ko
maqabarā yaha to kisī nūra jahāṃ kā bhī nahīṃ

✵ ✵ ✵

मेरी आंखों में.....

मेरी आंखों में कभी प्यार से झांका भी नहीं
वो जफ़ाकार[1] कि झूठा जो ज़ुबां का भी नहीं

जाने क्या सोच के दिल देती है दुनिया उसको
देखने में तो वो ऐसा कोई बांका भी नहीं

दिल दुखाने को न जाने वो किधर से आया?
रहने वाला वो मोहब्बत के जहां का भी नहीं

मैंने देखा नहीं अब तक किसी मौसम को सबात[2]
ग़म बहारों का नहीं है तो ख़िज़ाँ[3] का भी नहीं

क्यों भरे आह कोई देख के टूटे दिल को
मक़बरा यह तो किसी नूर जहां का भी नहीं

* * *

1. जफ़ा करने वाला 2. ठहराव 3. पतझड़

کھنکھناتے ہیں....

کھنکھناتے ہیں یوں تو جام بہت
سرد ہے میکدے کی شام بہت

جا چھپے اپنے اپنے کتبوں میں
تھی یہاں جن کی دھوم دھام بہت

اک مصوّر کو نیند آنے سے
رہ گئے نقش ناتمام بہت

زندگی اب تو روک ہاتھ اپنا
لے چکی ہم سے انتقام بہت

کتنا افسوس ہو رہا ہے قتیلؔ
عمر تھوڑی ہے اور کام بہت

* * *

THOUGH GOBLETS.....

Though goblets have a lot of resonance
Tavern in the evening has no effervescence

They are all hidden behind their epitaphs
Those seeking in the world permanence

An artist at work falling asleep
The painting remained without substance

O life, now you hold your hand
You have wrought lot of vengeance

What pity you feel, O "Qateel"
Life is short to go the distance

✸ ✸ ✸

Khankhanāte Haiṃ....

khanakhanāte haiṃ yūṁ to jāma bahuta
sarda hai mayakade kī śāma bahuta

jā chupe apane-apane kataboṃ meṃ
thī yahāṃ jinakī dhūma-dhāma bahuta

ika musavvira ko nīnda āne se
raha gae naqśa nā-tamāma bahuta

zindagī aba to roka hātha apanā
le cukī hama se iṃtaqāma bahuta

kitanā afasosa ho rahā hai "qatīla"
umra thoḍī hai aura kāma bahuta

* * *

खनखनाते हैं.....

खनखनाते हैं यूँ तो जाम बहुत
सर्द[1] है मयकदे की शाम बहुत

जा छुपे अपने–अपने कतबों[2] में
थी यहां जिनकी धूम–धाम बहुत

इक मुसव्विर[3] को नींद आने से
रह गए नक़्श[4] ना–तमाम[5] बहुत

ज़िंदगी अब तो रोक हाथ अपना
ले चुकी हम से इंतक़ाम[6] बहुत

कितना अफ़सोस हो रहा है "क़तील"
उम्र थोड़ी है और काम बहुत

* * *

---

1. ठण्डे 2. क़बर के ऊपर लगाने वाला पत्थर जिस पर मरने वाले के विषय में अंकित होता है 3. चित्रकार 4. चित्र 5. अपूर्ण 6. बदला

حکمراں مجھ کو بہاروں....

حکمراں مجھ کو بہاروں کا بنایا جائے
تاج کانٹوں کا مرے سر پہ سجایا جائے

ہر کوئی اب تو گنہ گار بنا بیٹھا ہے
پارسائی کا ہنر مجھ کو سکھایا جائے

موت برحق ہے مگر میری گزارش یہ ہے
زندہ انساں کا جنازہ نہ اٹھایا جائے

میں بتاؤں گا اُسے زخم کی لذت کیا ہے
پھول کا مجھ سے تعارف تو کرایا جائے

بڑھ گئی عمر مری نصف صدی سی بھی قتیلؔ
جشن اب میرے غموں کا بھی منایا جائے

❋ ❋ ❋

LET ME BECOME KING.....

Let me become king of spring
Crown of thorns on my head to bring

I may learn the ways of abstinence
Every one seems to be having a fling

Deat though inevitable, I have a plea
Please, no burial for anyone living

To flower I may be introduced
I shall explain to it the joy of sting

O "Qateel", I have exceeded half my life
Let us celebrate my woes of living

* * *

Hukmarām̐ Mujhko Bahāroṃ....

hukmarām̐ mujhako bahāroṃ kā banāyā jāe
tāja kāṇṭoṃ kā mire sara pe sajāyā jāe

hara koī aba to gunahagāra banā baiṭhā hai
pārasāī kā hunara mujha ko sikhāyā jāe

mauta barahaqa hai magara merī guzāriśa ye hai
zindā iṃsām̐ kā janāzā na uṭhāyā jāe

maiṃ batāūm̐gā use za<u>kh</u>ma kī lazzata kyā hai
phūla kā mujha se taārrufa to karāyā jāe

baḍ̂ha gaī umra mirī nisfa sadī se bhī "qatīla"
jaśna aba mere <u>gh</u>amoṃ kā bhī manāyā jāe

* * *

हुक्मराँ मुझको बहारों.....

हुक्मराँ[1] मुझको बहारों का बनाया जाए
ताज कांटों का मिरे सर पे सजाया जाए

हर कोई अब तो गुनहगार बना बैठा है
पारसाई[2] का हुनर मुझ को सिखाया जाए

मौत बरहक़[3] है मगर मेरी गुज़ारिश ये है
ज़िंदा इंसाँ का जनाज़ा न उठाया जाए

मैं बताऊँगा उसे ज़ख्म की लज़्ज़त[4] क्या है
फूल का मुझ से तआरुफ़[5] तो कराया जाए

बढ़ गई उम्र मिरी निस्फ़ सदी[6] से भी "क़तील"
जश्न अब मेरे ग़मों का भी मनाया जाए

* * *

1. शासक 2. नेक चलनी 3. सुनिश्चित 4. स्वाद 5. परिचय
6. आधी शताबदी

جب تک وہ جھومتا....

جب تک وہ جھومتا ہوا بادل نہ آئے گا
یارو کسی شجر پہ کبھی پھل نہ آئے گا

جب تک نہ اُس کے پاؤں کی زنجیر کاٹ دیں
محفل میں باندھ کر کوئی پائل نہ آئے گا

اَب آندھیاں چلیں گی ہواؤں کے نام پر
اَب راس دلبروں کو بھی آنچل نہ آئے گا

بہلا گیا وہ اپنی اداؤں سے آج بھی
وعدہ تو کر گیا ہے مگر کل نہ آئے گا

صدیاں تری سمیٹ کے جو لے گیا قتیلؔ
اب تیرے پاس لوٹ کے وہ پل نہ آئے گا

* * *

NOT UNTIL THAT CLOUD.....

Not until that cloud aloft will come
O friends, fruitful no tree will become

Not until we have cut fetters from the feet
No dancer with anklets in the enclave will come

Now breeze will turn into a stormy wind
Unbecoming beloved's apparel will become

Beloved today again has bemused with empty talks
Only an empty promise, tomorrow will become

The moment that encompassed many centuries past
having forsaken, for "Qateel" sake, it will not come

* * *

Jab Tak Vo Jhūmtā....

jaba taka vo jhūmatā huā bādala na āegā
yāro kisī śajara pe kabhī phala na āega

jaba taka na usake pām̐va kī zañjīra kāṭa deṃ
mahafila meṃ bāndha kara koī pāyala na āegā

aba āṃdhiyāṃ caleṅgī havāoṃ ke nāma para
aba rāsa dila baroṃ ko bhī ām̐cala na āegā

bahalā gayā vo apanī adāoṃ se āja bhī
vādā to kara gayā hai, magara kala na āegā

sadiyāṃ tirī asameṭa ke jo le gayā "qatīla"
aba tere pāsa lauṭa ke vo pala na āegā

✸ ✸ ✸

जब तक वो झूमता.....

जब तक वो झूमता हुआ बादल न आएगा
यारो किसी शजर[1] पे कभी फल न आएगा

जब तक न उसके पाँव की ज़ंजीर काट दें
महफ़िल में बांध कर कोई पायल न आएगा

अब आंधियां चलेंगी हवाओं के नाम पर
अब रास दिल बरों को भी आँचल न आएगा

बहला गया वो अपनी अदाओं से आज भी
वादा तो कर गया है, मगर कल न आएगा

सदियां तिरी समेट के जो ले गया "क़तील"
अब तेरे पास लौट के वो पल न आएगा

* * *

1. वृक्ष

تھوڑا سا غم....

تھوڑا سا غم ترکِ محبت ہے مجھے بھی
شرمندہ جو تُو ہے تو ندامت ہے مجھے بھی

میں تیری طرح دل کو سمجھتا نہیں شیشہ
ورنہ اسی دنیا سے شکایت ہے مجھے بھی

میں بھی ہوں اسی دَور کا سہما ہوا اِنساں
تھوڑے سے تبسّم کی ضرورت ہے مجھے بھی

جب زخم لگے، رقص کے انداز میں تڑپوں
قاتل کی طرف سے یہ ہدایت ہے مجھے بھی

فارغ ہو تو آجاؤ ذرا پیار ہی کرلیں
کچھ روز سے اِس کھیل کی فرصت ہے مجھے بھی

* * *

I ALSO SUFFER.....

I also suffer remorse for break in our relation
If you are put to shame, I have a sense of negation

I do not share your view that heart is meant for breaking
Against this world, otherwise, I have this inclination

I am, too, an oppressed being of the current era
I am, too, in need of a modicum of elation

When I am wounded, I am supposed to be ecstatic
My tormentor sends for me this signal and dictation

If you can spare some time, we can spar for love
I have time on hand for love, to hand this invitation

* * *

Thoḍā Sā Gham....

thoḍā sā ghame tarka-e-mohabbata hai mujhe bhī
śarmindā jo tū hai to nidāmata hai mujhe bhī

maiṃ terī taraha dila ko samajhatā nahīṃ śīśā
varnā isī duniyā se śikāyata hai mujhe bhī

maiṃ bhī hūm̐ isī daura kā sahamā huā iṃsām̐
thoḍe se tabassuma kī zarūrata hai mujhe bhī

jaba zakhma lage, raqsa ke aṃdāza meṃ taḍapūm̐
qātila kī tarafa se yaha hidāyata hai mujhe bhī

fārigha ho to ājāo zarā pyāra hī karaleṃ
kucha roza se isa khela kī fursata hai mujhe bhī

* * *

थोड़ा सा ग़म.....

थोड़ा सा ग़मे तर्क-ए-मोहब्बत[1] है मुझे भी
शर्मिंदा जो तू है तो निदामत[2] है मुझे भी

मैं तेरी तरह दिल को समझता नहीं शीशा
वर्ना इसी दुनिया से शिकायत है मुझे भी

मैं भी हूँ इसी दौर का सहमा हुआ इंसाँ
थोड़े से तबस्सुम[3] की ज़रूरत है मुझे भी

जब ज़ख़्म लगे, रक़्स[4] के अंदाज़ में तड़पूँ
क़ातिल की तरफ़ से यह हिदायत[5] है मुझे भी

फ़ारिग़[6] हो तो आजाओ ज़रा प्यार ही करलें
कुछ रोज़ से इस खेल की फ़ुर्सत है मुझे भी

✸ ✸ ✸

---

1. मोहब्बत छोड़ने का दुःख 2. शर्मिंदगी 3. मुस्कान 4. नाच
5. निर्देश 6. खाली, फुर्सत में

بات چھیڑ....

بات چھیڑ اس کے حسنِ جمیل کی
پھر دُعا مانگ عمرِ طویل کی

لے مزا تشنگی میں ثواب کا
آس رکھ کوثر و سلسبیل کی

کچھ نہ پائے گا اِس نامراد سے
زندگی ہے تجوری بخیل کی

سوچ لو عشق سے پہلے عاشقو
پیٹ بھرنے کی بھی کچھ سبیل کی

ڈٹ گیا چشم و ابرو کے سامنے
قاتلوں سے ٹھنی ہے قتیل کی

* * *

TALK OF BELOVED'S.....

Talk of beloved's beauty inordinate
Then pray for your life to reincarnate

Take pleasure in reward for abstinence
In after life hope and wait

You find nothing from this stingy source
Life's coffers are empty to date

O lovers look before you leap
Body with soul should be intimate

"Qateel" is looking beloved in face
unafraid to face his fate

* * *

Bāt Cheḍ....

bāta cheḍa usake husna-e-jamīla kī
phira duā māṅga umra-e-tavīla kī

le mazā tiśnagī meṃ savāba kā
āsa rakha kausara-o-sala sabīla kī

kucha na pāegā isa nāmurāda se
zindagī hai tijorī ba<u>kh</u>īla kī

soca lo iśqa se pahale āśiqoṃ
peṭa bharane kī bhī kucha sabīla kī

ḍaṭa gayā caśma-o-abu ke sāmane
qātiloṃ se ṭhanī hai "qatīla" kī

* * *

बात छेड़.....

बात छेड़ उसके हुस्न-ए-जमील[1] की
फिर दुआ मांग उम्र-ए-तवील[2] की

ले मज़ा तिश्नगी[3] में सवाब का
आस रख कौसर-ओ-सल सबील[4] की

कुछ न पाएगा इस नामुराद से
ज़िंदगी है तिजोरी बख़ील[5] की

सोच लो इश्क़ से पहले आशिक़ो
पेट भरने की भी कुछ सबील[6] की

डट गया चश्म-ओ-अब्रु के सामने
क़ातिलों से ठनी है "क़तील" की

* * *

1. सुन्दरता 2. दीर्घायु 3. प्यास 4. स्वर्ग में बहने वाली शराब की नहरें 5. कंजूस 6. उपाय

اُن کے بغیر جی....

اُن کے بغیر جی تو رہے ہیں قتیلؔ ہم
کرلیں نہ بے مزا کہیں عمرِ طویل ہم

آئیں گے اپنے بعد بھی کچھ رہروانِ شوق
رستے میں گاڑ دو کہ بنیں سنگِ میل ہم

دم گھُٹ رہا تھا شہرِ ندامت میں دوستو
پھاند آئے احتیاط کی اونچی فصیل ہم

دَر پر لگا ہے قفل تو روزن ہی کھول دے
تازہ ہواؤں میں تو رہیں خود کفیل، ہم

سات آسماں ہیں راستہ روکے ہوئے قتیلؔ
آخر کہاں سے لائیں پرِ جبرئیل ہم

* * *

WITHOUT BELOVED.....

Without beloved, though O "Qateel", we are living
Our long life we may be passing without a fling

Some eager trekkers will come, after we are gone
We may become a landmark for the future swing

We were feeling suffocated in the guarded citadel
We jumped over the high wall to escape arrows and sling

If the door is locked, let windows be opened
So we are self sufficient in fresh air's swing

Seven heavens in our way are at sixes and sevens
How alas, O "Qateel", to borrow an angel's wing

* * *

Unke Ba<u>gh</u>air Jī....

unake ba<u>gh</u>aira jī to rahe haiṃ "qatīla" hama
karaleṃ na be mazā kahīṃ umra-e-tavīla hama

āeṃge apane bāda bhī kucha raharavāna-e-śauqa
raste meṃ gāḓa do ki bane saṅga-e-mīla hama

dama ghuṭa rahā thā śahra-e-nidāmata meṃ dosto
phānda āe ehatiyāta kī ūm̐cī fasīla hama

dara para lagā hai qufla to rozana hī khola de
tāzā havāoṃ meṃ to raheṃ <u>kh</u>uda-kafīla hama

sāta āsmāṃ haiṃ rāstā roke hue "qatīla"
ā<u>kh</u>ira kahām̐ se lāeṃ para-e-jibarāīla hama

* * *

उनके बग़ैर जी.....

उनके बग़ैर जी तो रहे हैं "क़तील" हम
करलें न बे मज़ा कहीं उम्र-ए-तवील[1] हम

आएंगे अपने बाद भी कुछ रहरवान-ए-शौक़[2]
रस्ते में गाड़ दो कि बने संग-ए-मील[3] हम

दम घुट रहा था शह्र-ए-निदामत[4] में दोस्तो
फांद आए एहतियात की ऊँची फ़सील[5] हम

दर पर लगा है क़ुफ़्ल[6] तो रोज़न[7] ही खोल दे
ताज़ा हवाओं में तो रहें खुद-कफ़ील[8] हम

सात आस्मां हैं रास्ता रोके हुए "क़तील"
आखिर कहाँ से लाएं पर-ए-जिबरईल[9] हम

* * *

---

1. लम्बी आयु 2. प्यार करने के राही 3. रास्ते की दूरी बताने वाला पत्थर 4. शर्मिंदगी 5. दीवार 6. ताला 7. खिड़की, झरोखा 8. आत्म निर्भर 9. खुदा के दूत जो अपने परों से उड़ते हुए नबियों (अवतारों) तक खुदा के संदेश लाया करते थे

حالات کے قدموں پہ....

حالات کے قدموں پہ قلندر نہیں گرتا
ٹوٹے بھی جو تارا تو زمیں پر نہیں گرتا

گرتے ہیں سمندر میں بڑے شوق سے دریا
لیکن کسی دریا میں سمندر نہیں گرتا

سمجھو وہاں پھل دار شجر کوئی نہیں ہے
وہ صحن کہ جس میں کوئی پتھر نہیں گرتا

اِتنا تو ہوا فائدہ بارش کی کمی سے
اس شہر میں اب کوئی پھسل کر نہیں گرتا

حیراں ہے کئی روز سے ٹھہرا ہوا پانی
تالاب میں اب کیوں کوئی کنکر نہیں گرتا

* * *

A DAUNTLESS PERSON.....

A dauntless person is not beaten by circumstance
A star falling from sky does not accept earthly stance

Rivers flow without ado to merge with the ocean
Ocean, though, for the rivers makes no advance

A fruit bearing tree is surely not there
If it does not attract a stone even by a chance

Scracity of rainfall has its own effect
No one in the town slips down perchance

Why no pebble has disturbed stillness of the pond
For many a day it has been in a state of trans

* * *

Hālāt Ke Qadmoṃ Pe....

hālāta ke qadamoṃ pe qalandara nahīṃ giratā
ṭūṭe bhī jo tārā to zamīṃ para nahīṃ giratā

girate haiṃ samandara meṃ baḍe śauqa se dariyā
lekina kisī dariyā meṃ samandara nahīṃ giratā

samajho vahāṃ phaladāra śajara koī nahīṃ hai
vo sahna kī jisa meṃ koī patthara nahīṃ giratā

itanā to huā fāyedā bāriśa kī kamī se
isa śahra meṃ aba koī phisala kara nahīṃ giratā

hairāṁ hai kaī roza se ṭhaharā huā pānī
tālāba meṃ aba kyoṃ koī kaṅkara nahīṃ giratā

* * *

हालात के क़दमों पे.....

हालात के क़दमों पे क़लंदर[1] नहीं गिरता
टूटे भी जो तारा तो ज़मीं पर नहीं गिरता

गिरते हैं समन्दर में बड़े शौक़ से दरिया
लेकिन किसी दरिया में समन्दर नहीं गिरता

समझो वहां फलदार शजर[2] कोई नहीं है
वो सहन कि जिस में कोई पत्थर नहीं गिरता

इतना तो हुआ फ़ायदा बारिश की कमी से
इस शहर में अब कोई फिसल कर नहीं गिरता

हैराँ है कई रोज़ से ठहरा हुआ पानी
तालाब में अब क्यों कोई कंकर नहीं गिरता

* * *

---

1. मस्त, सन्त   2. वृक्ष

ہوئی نہ راہ میں حائل....

ہوئی نہ راہ میں حائل شکستہ پائی مری
قتیلؔ اب بھی ہے اک شخص تک رسائی مری

اُچھالتے ہیں مرے ذکر سے وہ نام اپنا
پسند ہے مرے یاروں کو ہر برائی مری

اب اور لوگوں میں جائے وہ غم غلط کرنے
سنا ہے اس کو گوارا نہیں جُدائی مری

بس ایک بار شکن پڑگئی تھی ماتھے پر
منانے مجھ کو جوانی کبھی نہ آئی مری

قتیلؔ شکر کروں، جب بھی مجھ پہ تیر چلے
بہ فیضِ عشق، طبیعت ہے کربلائی مری

* * *

WEARINESS OF MY FEET.....

Weariness of my feet could not at all deter
My access to the beloved, as my feet are still astir

They elevate their fame, by mentioning my name
With every oversight of mine, my well wishers infer

Let my beloved go somewhere else for solace
As my company beloved is heard to prefer

Furrow on my forehead once it had appeared
My youthfulness did not look back to defer

O "Qateel" I am thankful for ever glancing arrow
Thanks to love's indulgence, my soul to bestir

* * *

Huī Na Rāh Meṃ Hāil....

huī na rāha meṃ hāila śakistā-pāī mirī
"qatīla" aba bhī hai ika śa<u>kh</u>sa taka rāsaī mirī

uchālate haiṃ mire zikra se vo nāma apanā
pasanda hai mire yāroṃ ko hara burāī mirī

aba aura logoṃ meṃ jāe vo <u>gh</u>ama <u>gh</u>alata karane
sunā hai usako gavārā nahīṃ judāī mirī

basa eka bāra śikana pad̂a gaī thī māthe para
manāne mujha ko javānī kabhī na āī mirī

"qatīla" śukra karūm̐, jaba bhī mujha pe tīra cale
ba-faiza-e-iśqa tabīyata hai karabalāī mirī

✹ ✹ ✹

हुई न राह में हाइल.....

हुई न राह में हाइल[1] शकिस्ता–पाई[2] मिरी
"क़तील" अब भी है इक शख्स तक रसाई[3] मिरी

उछालते हैं मिरे ज़िक्र से वो नाम अपना
पसंद है मिरे यारों को हर बुराई मिरी

अब और लोगों में जाए वो ग़म ग़लत करने
सुना है उसको गवारा नहीं जुदाई मिरी

बस एक बार शिकन पड़ गई थी माथे पर
मनाने मुझ को जवानी कभी न आई मिरी

"क़तील" शुक्र करूँ, जब भी मुझ पे तीर चले
ब–फ़ैज़–ए–इश्क़ तबीयत है करबलाई[5] मिरी

* * *

---

1. रुकावट 2. टूटी हुई चाल 3. पहुँच 4. इश्क़ की बदौलत, इश्क़ के चमत्कार से 5. करबला वालों की तरह जवां मर्दी से तीरों को अपने सीने पर झेलने वाला स्वभाव

زندگی کے غم لاکھوں....

زندگی کے غم لاکھوں اور چشمِ نم تنہا
حسرتوں کی میّت پر رو رہے ہیں ہم تنہا

مل سکا نہ کوئی بھی ہم سفر زمانے میں
کاٹتے رہے برسوں جادۂ الم تنہا

کھیل تو نہیں یارو راستے کی تنہائی
کوئی ہم کو دکھلائے چل کے دو قدم تنہا

دِل کو چھیڑتی ہوگی یادِ رفتگاں اکثر
لاکھ جی کو بہلائیں شیخِ محترم تنہا

تھی قتیلؔ چاہت میں ان کی بھی رضا شامل
پھر بھی ہم ہی ٹھہرے ہیں موردِ ستم تنہا

* * *

MILLION WOES OF LIFE.....

Million woes of life and weeping eye alone
On the demise of longings, we are weeping on our own

We could not find in the world any one's company
We trekked the path of woes all along all alone

To go on our way it is not child's play
Let any one show us a step or two alone

Nostalgia of the youth must be tormenting
Preacher may try to muse or to atone

O "Qateel" beloved was equally to blame
Even then we have to stand to suffer all alone

* * *

Zindagī Ke G͟ham Lākhoṃ....

zindagī ke g͟hama lākhoṃ aura caśma-e-nama tanhā
hasaratoṃ kī mayyata para ro rahe haiṃ hama tanhā

mila sakā na koī bhī hama safara zamāne meṃ
kāṭate rahe barasoṃ jādā-e-alama tanhā

khela to nahīṃ yāro rāste kī tanhāī
koī hamako dikhalāe cala ke do qadama tanhā

dila ko cheḓatī hogī yāda-e-raftagāṃ aksara
lākha jī ko bahalāeṃ śek͟ha-e-mohatarama tanhā

thī "qatīla" cāhata meṃ unakī bhī razā śāmila
phira bhī hama hī ṭhahare haiṃ mūrida-e-sitama tanhā

* * *

ज़िंदगी के ग़म लाखों.....

ज़िंदगी के ग़म लाखों और चश्म–ए–नम[1] तन्हा
हसरतों की मय्यत पर रो रहे हैं हम तन्हा

मिल सका न कोई भी हम सफ़र ज़माने में
काटते रहे बरसों जादा–ए–अलम[2] तन्हा

खेल तो नहीं यारो रास्ते की तन्हाई
कोई हमको दिखलाए चल के दो क़दम तन्हा

दिल को छेड़ती होगी याद–ए–रफ़्तगां[3] अक्सर
लाख जी को बहलाएं शेख–ए–मोहतरम तन्हा

थी "क़तील" चाहत में उनकी भी रज़ा शामिल
फिर भी हम ही ठहरे हैं मूरिद–ए–सितम[4] तन्हा

* * *

---

1. भीगी आंख 2. दुःख का रास्ता 3. अतीत की याद
4. अत्याचार का शिकार

دُور تک چھائے تھے بادل....

دُور تک چھائے تھے بادل اور کہیں سایہ نہ تھا
اس طرح برسات کا موسم کبھی آیا نہ تھا

کیا ملا آخر تجھے سایوں کے پیچھے بھاگ کر
اے دلِ ناداں، تجھے کیا ہم نے سمجھایا نہ تھا

اُف یہ سنّاٹا کہ آہٹ تک نہ ہو جس میں مخل
زندگی میں اس قدر ہم نے سکوں پایا نہ تھا

خُوب روئے چھپ کے گھر کی چار دیواری میں ہم
حالِ دل کہنے کے قابل کوئی ہمسایا نہ تھا

صرف خوشبُو کی کمی تھی موسمِ گل میں قتیلؔ
ورنہ گلشن میں کوئی بھی پھوُل مرجھایا نہ تھا

* * *

THEY WERE CLOUDS.....

There were clouds galore, yet shade was non existent
Rainy season such as this was never so inconsistent

What, after all, you had gained chasing shadows
O wayward heart, we had asked no to be insistent

Ah this solitude, not a sound to intrude
In our life such quietude was never so persistent

In the four walls of home, we had cried on own
To tell our tale of woe, we found neighbours distant

Flowers were aplenty, scent, though, was scanty
Things otherwise, in the garden were so efflorescent

* * *

Dūr Tak Chāe The Bādal....

dūra taka chāe the bādala aura kahīṃ sāyā na thā
isa taraha barasāta kā mausama kabhī āyā na thā

kyā milā ākhira tujhe sāyoṃ ke pīche bhāgakara
ai dila-e-nādāṃ, tujhe kyā hamane samajhāyā na thā

ufa ye sannāṭā ki āhaṭa taka na ho jisameṃ mukhila
zindagī meṃ isa qadara hamane sakūṁ pāyā na thā

khūba roe chupa ke ghara kī cāra dīvārī meṃ hama
hāla-e-dila kahane ke qābila koī hamasāyā na thā

sirfa khuśbū kī kamī thī mausama-e-gula meṃ "qatīla"
varnā gulaśana meṃ koī bhī phūla murjhāyā na thā

✸ ✸ ✸

दूर तक छाए थे बादल.....

दूर तक छाए थे बादल और कहीं साया न था
इस तरह बरसात का मौसम कभी आया न था

क्या मिला आख़िर तुझे सायों के पीछे भागकर
ऐ दिल-ए-नादां, तुझे क्या हमने समझाया न था

उफ़ ये सन्नाटा कि आहट तक न हो जिसमें मुख़िल[1]
ज़िंदगी में इस क़दर हमने सकूँ पाया न था

ख़ूब रोए छुप के घर की चार दीवारी में हम
हाल-ए-दिल कहने के क़ाबिल कोई हमसाया[2] न था

सिर्फ़ ख़ुश्बू की कमी थी मौसम-ए-गुल में "क़तील"
वर्ना गुलशन में कोई भी फूल मुर्झाया न था

* * *

---

1. हस्तक्षेप करना 2. पड़ोसी

جب سے اسیر زلف....

جب سے اسیرِ زلفِ گرہ گیر ہو گیا
میں بے نیازِ حلقۂ زنجیر ہو گیا

جاتا کہاں بھلا تری محفل کو چھوڑ کر
میں آپ اپنے پاؤں کی زنجیر ہو گیا

نورِ جہاں کوئی نہ کوئی یوں تو سبکی تھی
دولت سے ایک شخص جہانگیر ہو گیا

مجھ میں رچی ہوئی تری خوشبو تھی اس لئے
بڑھ کر عدو بھی مجھ سے بغل گیر ہو گیا

پھر باندھ لی کسی سے امیدِ وفا قتیلؔ
پھر اک محل ہواؤں میں تعمیر ہو گیا

* * *

EVER SINCE.....

Ever since I have been prisoner of beloved's tassel
I am so indifferent to the fetter's hassel

Where could I go leaving your enclave
I myself became a chain around my own ankle

Empress Noor Jehan was a queen of hearts
Emperor Jehangir was, with his wealth, a debacle

Beloved had imbibed such qualities in me
For the rival, my ettiquette became quite acceptable

Once again, O "Qateel", I trusted beloved's promise
Once again, in the air, I had built a castle

* * *

Jab Se Asīr-E-Zulf....

jaba se asīra-e-zulfa-e-giraha gīra ho gayā
maiṃ be-niyāza-e-halqā-e-zañjīra ho gayā

jātā kahāṃ bhalā tirī mahafila ko choḍakara
maiṃ āpa apane pām̐va kī zañjīra ho gayā

nūra-e-jahāṃ koī na koī yūm̐ to sabakī thī
daulata se eka śak͟hsa jahāṅgīra ho gayā

mujha meṃ racī huī tirī k͟huśbū thī isalie
baḍhakara adū bhī mujhase bag͟halagīra ho gayā

phira bāndha lī kisī se ummīda-e-vafā "qatīla"
phira ika mahala havāoṃ meṃ tāmīra ho gayā

✸ ✸ ✸

जब से असीर-ए-ज़ुल्फ.....

जब से असीर–ए–ज़ुल्फ़–ए–गिरह गीर[1] हो गया
मैं बे–नियाज़–ए–हल्क़ा–ए–ज़ंजीर[2] हो गया

जाता कहां भला तिरी महफ़िल को छोड़कर
मैं आप अपने पाँव की ज़ंजीर हो गया

नूर–ए–जहां कोई न कोई यूँ तो सबकी थी
दौलत से एक शख़्स जहांगीर हो गया

मुझ में रची हुई तिरी खुश्बू थी इसलिए
बढ़कर अदू[3] भी मुझसे बग़लगीर[4] हो गया

फिर बांध ली किसी से उम्मीद–ए–वफ़ा "क़तील"
फिर इक महल हवाओं में तामीर[5] हो गया

* * *

---

1. घुंघराले बालों का क़ैदी, ज़ंजीर (क़ैद की चिंता से मुक्त)
3. दुश्मन 4. गले मिलना 5. निर्माण

وہ شخص کہ میں جس سے....

وہ شخص کہ میں جس سے محبت نہیں کرتا
ہنستا ہے مجھے دیکھ کے نفرت نہیں کرتا

پکڑا ہی گیا ہوں تو مجھے دار پہ کھینچو
سچّا ہوں مگر اپنی وکالت نہیں کرتا

گھر والوں کو غفلت پہ سبھی کوس رہے ہیں
چوروں کو مگر کوئی ملامت نہیں کرتا

دیتے ہیں اُجالے مرے سجدوں کی گواہی
میں چھُپ کے اندھیروں میں عبادت نہیں کرتا

دنیا میں قتیلؔ اُس سا منافق نہیں کوئی
جو ظلم تو سہتا ہے بغاوت نہیں کرتا

* * *

A PERSON FOR WHOM.....

A person for whom I show no love expression
He is amused seeing without any repulsion

Now that I am caught, you hang me high
I am, though, truthful, I offer no explanation

Everyone is scolding for the owner's neglect
For the thief, though, no one shows repulsion

I do not got to pray in hours of darkness
Light of dawn is witness to my supplication

In the world, O "Qateel", no worse an hypocrite
Who does not rise to rebel, yet suffers all oppression

* * *

Vo Śakhs Ki Maiṃ Jisse....

vo śakhsa ki maiṃ jisase mohabbata nahīṃ karatā
haṃsatā hai mujhe dekha ke nafarata nahīṃ karatā

pakaḍā hī gayā hūṁ to mujhe dāra pe khīñco
saccā hūṁ magara apanī vakālata nahīṃ karatā

ghara vāloṃ ko ghafalata pe sabhī kosa rahe haiṃ
coroṃ ko magara koī malāmata nahīṃ karatā

dete haiṃ ujāle mire sijadoṃ kī gavāhī
maiṃ chupa ke aṃdheroṃ meṃ ibādata nahīṃ karatā

duniyā meṃ "qatīla" usa sā munāfiqa nahīṃ koī
jo zulma to sahatā hai baghāvata nahīṃ karatā

* * *

वो शख़्स कि मैं जिससे.....

वो शख्स कि मैं जिससे मोहब्बत नहीं करता
हंसता है मुझे देख के नफ़रत नहीं करता

पकड़ा ही गया हूँ तो मुझे दार[1] पे खींचो
सच्चा हूँ मगर अपनी वकालत नहीं करता

घर वालों को ग़फ़लत पे सभी कोस रहे हैं
चोरों को मगर कोई मलामत नहीं करता

देते हैं उजाले मिरे सिजदों की गवाही
मैं छुप के अंधेरों में इबादत नहीं करता

दुनिया में "क़तील" उस सा मुनाफ़िक[2] नहीं कोई
जो जुल्म तो सहता है बग़ावत नहीं करता

* * *

1. फांसी 2. औरों का बुरा चाहने वाला

جب اس کے پاس مرا....

جب اس کے پاس مرا نامہ بَر گیا ہوگا
تمام بزم کا چہرہ اُتر گیا ہوگا

یقیں تھا شیخ کو جنّت میں جام کھنکیں گے
اِسی خوشی میں وہ پیاسا ہی مر گیا ہوگا

تڑپ رہے ہیں یہ کیوں مجھ سمیت دل والے
کسی کا تیرِ نظر کام کرگیا ہوگا

تمہارے دَر سے پلٹ آیا جو دبے پاؤں
وہ شخص وعدۂ فردا سے ڈر گیا ہوگا

سُنا ہے لُٹ گئے رستے میں قافلے والے
ضرور ساتھ کوئی راہبر گیا ہوگا

* * *

WHEN MY MESSAGE....

When my message bearer had delivered beloved my letter
The whole enclave would be envious in the matter

He would have kept himself in the thirst in this world
The preacher was for next world sure of heavenly nectar

Beloved's glancing arrow would have been effective
Every one including myself would have been in tatter

The person who from your door returned incognito
For your promise of tomorrow, he had wished to flatter

It is heard that the caravan was looted on the way
It must have been accompanied by a leader meant to scatter

* * *

Jab Uske Pās Mirā...

jaba usake pāsa mirā nāmābara gayā hogā
tamāma bazma kā ceharā utara gayā hogā

yaqīṃ thā śai<u>kh</u>a ko jannata meṃ jāma khanakeṅge
isī <u>kh</u>uśī meṃ vo pyāsā hī mara gayā hogā

tad̂apa rahe haiṃ ye kyoṃ mujha sameta dila vāle
kisī kā tīra-e-nazara kāma kara gayā hogā

tumhâre dara se palaṭa āyā jo dabe pām̐va
vo śa<u>kh</u>sa vādā-e-fardā se ḍara gayā hogā

sunā hai luṭa gae raste meṃ qāfile vāle
zarūra sātha koī rāhabara gayā hogā

* * *

जब उसके पास मिरा.....

जब उसके पास मिरा नामाबर[1] गया होगा
तमाम बज़्म[2] का चेहरा उतर गया होगा

यक़ीं था शैख़ को जन्नत में जाम खनकेंगे
इसी ख़ुशी में वो प्यासा ही मर गया होगा

तड़प रहे हैं ये क्यों मुझ समेत दिल वाले
किसी का तीर-ए-नज़र काम कर गया होगा

तुम्हारे दर से पलट आया जो दबे पाँव
वो शख़्स वादा-ए-फ़र्दा[3] से डर गया होगा

सुना है लुट गए रस्ते में क़ाफ़िले वाले
ज़रूर साथ कोई राहबर गया होगा

* * *

---

1. पत्र वाहक 2. महफ़िल 3. कल का वादा

سوچا تھا اپنے آپ....

سوچا تھا اپنے آپ سے شاید سبق ملے
کورے کتابِ عمر کے سارے ورق ملے

ہم پر کوئی نصاب نہ تھا آج تک گراں
اَب کے مگر بہت سے مضامیں ادق ملے

بے سمت منزلوں کو رواں تھا وہ راہبر
چہرے تمام قافلے والوں کے فق ملے

بین السّطور جن کی تباہی کا ذکر ہے
یارَب انہیں بھی حرف شناسی کا حق ملے

اُس شخص کی تلاش ہے اب تک مجھے قتیؔل
ایمان کی ذراسی بھی جس میں رمق ملے

* * *

WE THOUGHT.....

We thought we may learn from own life's experience
All leaves in life's book were blank in appearance

No text book was ever found difficult so far
But many a new subject was hard for persevereance

Leader of the caravan had lost sense of direction
Faces of all trekkers were pale in every sense

Whose ever ruin is mentioned in between the lines
they may be given credit for their disappearance

O "Qateel", I am in search of that very person
Who allowed lack of faith no interference

✹ ✹ ✹

Socā Thā Apne Āp....

socā thā apane āpa se śāyada sabaqa mile
kore kitāba-e-umra ke sāre varaqa mile

hama para koī nisāba na thā āja taka girām̐
aba ke magara bahuta se mazāmī adaqa mile

be-simta mañziloṃ ko ravāṃ thā vo rāhabara
cahare tamāma qāfile vāloṃ ke faqa mile

baina-usa-satūra jinakī tabāhī kā zikra hai
yā raba unheṃ bhī harfa śanāsī kā haqa mile

usa śakhsa kī talāśa hai aba taka mujhe "qatīla"
īmāna kī zarā sī bhī jisameṃ ramaqa mile

* * *

सोचा था अपने आप.....

सोचा था अपने आप से शायद सबक़ मिले
कोरे किताब-ए-उम्र के सारे वरक़ मिले

हम पर कोई निसाब[1] न था आज तक गिराँ
अब के मगर बहुत से मज़ामीं[2] अदक़[3] मिले

बे-सिम्त[4] मंज़िलों को रवां था वो राहबर
चहरे तमाम क़ाफ़िले वालों के फ़क़ मिले

बैन-उस-सतूर जिनकी तबाही का ज़िक्र है
या रब उन्हें भी हर्फ़ शनासी का हक़ मिले

उस शख़्स की तलाश है अब तक मुझे "क़तील"
ईमान की ज़रा सी भी जिसमें रमक़[6] मिले

* * *

---

1. सिलेबस 2. विषय 3. कठिन 4. दिशा हीन 5. दो लाइनों के बीच का अन्तर 6. चमक

ترے گلے میں اگر....

ترے گلے میں اگر موتیوں کی مالا ہے
یہ سوچ کس نے مکان اپنا بیچ ڈالا ہے

ہمیشہ جھوٹ ہم آپس میں بولتے آئے
نہ میرے دل میں نہ تیری زباں پہ چھالا ہے

جو سب نے دیکھ لیا میں بھی اُس کو دیکھ سکوں
کوئی بتائے وہ کس رنگ کا اُجالا ہے

کتابِ عمر نہ چھپوا سکا میں آج تلک
کہ ہر ورق پہ ترے نام کا حوالہ ہے

نہیں ضرور کہ ہو پیار ایک بار قتیلؔ
یہ میٹھا روگ کئی بار ہم نے پالا ہے

* * *

IF AROUND YOUR NECK.....

If around your neck is diamond studded necklace
Just think of the bankruptcy someone to face

We treated each other with a pace of lies
In my heart, on your tongue, no sense of disgrace

I would love to see what everyone has seen
Let someone at least enlighten me as to colour base

I could not till today get autobiography published
On every page is inscribed your name and preface

It is not essential, O "Qateel" to love only once
This pleasant malady many a time we were to embrace

* * *

Tire Gale Meṃ Agar....

tire gale meṃ agara motiyoṃ kī mālā hai
yaha soca kisane makāna apanā beca ḍālā hai

hameśā jhūṭha hama āpasa meṃ bolate āe
na mere dila meṃ na terī zubā̃ṁ pe chālā hai

jo sabane dekha liyā maiṃ bhī usako dekha sakū̃ṁ
koī batāe vo kisa raṅga kā ujālā hai

kitāba-e-umra na chapavā sakā maiṃ āja talaka
ki hara varaqa pe tire nāma kā havālā hai

nahīṃ zarūra ki ho pyāra eka bāra "qatīla"
ye mīṭhā roga kaī bāra hamane pālā hai

* * *

तिरे गले में अगर.....

तिरे गले में अगर मोतियों की माला है
यह सोच किसने मकान अपना बेच डाला है

हमेशा झूठ हम आपस में बोलते आए
न मेरे दिल में न तेरी ज़ुबाँ पे छाला है

जो सबने देख लिया मैं भी उसको देख सकूँ
कोई बताए वो किस रंग का उजाला है

किताब–ए–उम्र[1] न छपवा सका मैं आज तलक
कि हर वरक़ पे तिरे नाम का हवाला है

नहीं ज़रूर कि हो प्यार एक बार "क़तील"
ये मीठा रोग कई बार हमने पाला है

* * *

1. जीवन की पुस्तक

لُوٹا جو ہمسفر نے....

لُوٹا جو ہمسفر نے تو نوچا لباس بھی
ایسا تو بے لحاظ کوئی راہزن نہ تھا

مقتل میں یوں تو تھے شہداء ملک کے
لاشہ کسی کا میری طرح بے کفن نہ تھا

مانگی تھی میں نے شہریتِ خلد اس لئے
رُوئے زمین پر میرا کوئی وطن نہ تھا

ریشم کے جس لباس پہ نازاں تھا ایک شخص
دیکھا تو اُس لباس کے اندر بدن نہ تھا

اُس ابرِ نوبہار کی اُمید میں قتیلؔ
میں دشتِ انتظار میں کب خیمہ زن نہ تھا

✹ ✹ ✹

THE FELLOW TRAVELLER....

The fellow traveller looted, shredded apparel as well
Never had any pirate shown such ruthlessness

On the field of battle, martyrs remained piles deep
Unlike my remains, none had suffered shroudlessness

I had asked for citizenship in the high heaven
In the Netherland I was in a state of statelessness

A person was so proud of his silken raiment
Upon close examination, it was such

In the hope of cloudburst of the early spring
I had waited, O "Qateel", in vain, in hopelessness

* * *

Lūṭā Jo Ham Safar....

lūṭā jo hama safara ne to nocā libāsa bhī
aisā to be lihāza koī rāhazana na thā

maqatala meṃ yūm̐ to the śohdā mulka-mulka ke
lāśā kisī kā merī taraha be kafana na thā

māṅgī thī mainne śahariyata-e-khulda isa lie
rū-e-zamīna pe merā koī bhī vatana na thā

reśama ke jisa libāsa pe nāzāṃ thā eka śakhsa
dekhā to usa libāsa ke aṃdara badana na thā

usa abra-e-naubahāra kī ummīda meṃ "qatīla"
maiṃ daśta-e-intizāra meṃ kaba khemā-zana na thā

* * *

लूटा जो हम सफ़र.....

लूटा जो हम सफ़र ने तो नोचा लिबास भी
ऐसा तो बे लिहाज़ कोई राहज़न न था

मक़तल[1] में यूँ तो थे शोहदा[2] मुल्क-मुल्क के
लाशा किसी का मेरी तरह बे कफ़न न था

मांगी थी मैंने शहरियत-ए-ख़ुल्द[3] इस लिए
रू-ए-ज़मीन पे मेरा कोई भी वतन न था

रेशम के जिस लिबास पे नाज़ाँ[4] था एक शख़्स
देखा तो उस लिबास के अंदर बदन न था

उस अब्र-ए-नौबहार[5] की उम्मीद में "क़तील"
मैं दश्त-ए-इन्तिज़ार[6] में कब ख़ैमा-ज़न[7] न था

* * *

---

1. क़त्ल होने का स्थान 2. शहीद 3. स्वर्ग की नागरिकता 4. गर्व करना 5. नई बहार के मौसम का बादल 6. इन्तिज़ार का जंगल 7. पड़ाव डाले हुए

شبِ وصال کچھ ایسا....

شبِ وصال کچھ ایسا نکھر رہا تھا کوئی
خود اپنے حُسن کو حیران کررہا تھا کوئی

وہ مجھ سے دُور تھا، میں پھر بھی لڑکھڑاسا گیا
خمار بن کے بدن میں اُتر رہا تھا کوئی

وہ جلد کیسے پہنچتا لبوں کے ساحل پر
سمندروں کی تہوں سے اُبھر رہا تھا کوئی

ضرور نصب وہاں کوئی آئینہ ہوگا
نظر جھکائے جہاں سے گزر رہا تھا کوئی

قتیلؔ مجھ کو بُرا اُس نے کہہ دیا بھی تو کیا؟
یہی بہت ہے مجھے یاد کررہا تھا کوئی

* * *

ON THE NIGHT.....

On the night of union, beloved was resplendent
Beauty, even though, wonder struck was itself ascendent

Though from beloved not so near, I was struck with fear
I was feeling drowsy, ever so dependent

How could I dare to reach beloved's lips there
Fathoms deep though, I was feeling buoyant

There must be a mirror somewhere in the vicinity
Not without indignity, rival was ambivalent

O "Qateel", no ill feeling if beloved was unfeeling
To be remembered with some feeling, I was triumphant

* * *

Śab-E-Visāl Kuch Aisā....

śaba-e-visāla kucha aisā nikhara rahā thā koī
khuda apane husna ko hairāna kara rahā thā koī

vo mujhase dūra thā, maiṃ phira abhī laḋakhaḋā sā gayā
khumāra banake badana meṃ utara rahā thā koī

vo jalda kaise pahum̐catā laboṃ ke asāhila para
samandaroṃ kī tahoṃ se ubhara rahā thā koī

zarūra nasba vahāṃ koī āīnā hogā
nazara jhukāe jahāṃ se guzara rahā thā koī

"qatīla" mujhako burā usane kaha diyā bhī to kyā?
yahī bahuta hai mujhe yāda kara rahā thā koī

* * *

शब-ए-विसाल कुछ ऐसा....

शब–ए–विसाल[1] कुछ ऐसा निखर रहा था कोई
खुद अपने हुस्न को हैरान कर रहा था कोई

वो मुझसे दूर था, मैं फिर भी लड़खड़ा सा गया
खुमार[2] बनके बदन में उतर रहा था कोई

वो जल्द कैसे पहुँचता लबों[3] के साहिल पर
समन्दरों की तहों से उभर रहा था कोई

ज़रूर नरब वहां कोई आईना होगा
नज़र झुकाए जहां से गुज़र रहा था कोई

"क़तील" मुझको बुरा उसने कह दिया भी तो क्या?
यही बहुत है मुझे याद कर रहा था कोई

* * *

---

1. मिलन की रात 2. नशा 3. होठों 4. लगाना

تمام شہر کے رستے....

تمام شہر کے رستے سجادیے جائیں
ہم آگئے ہیں تو کانٹے بچھادیے جائیں

ہمیں سکون سے اِک دن قیام کرنا ہے
زمیں پہ دُھوپ کے خیمے لگادیے جائیں

ابھی تلک جو خموشی میں ڈالتے ہیں خلل
درخت سے وہ پرندے اڑادیے جائیں

مبادا رات چلی آئے شام سے پہلے
چراغ کیوں نہ ابھی سے بُجھادیے جائیں

قتیلؔ اپنے لئے وہ کشش زمین میں ہے
یہیں گریں گے جہاں سے گرادیے جائیں

* * *

LET ALL THE STREETS.....

Let all the streets with thorns be decorated
Now that we have come, let feet be perforated

We wish one day to have peace and quiet
Let earth with scorching sun be incinerated

Whichever birds infringe on trees solitude
From the trees, let them be expatriated

Lest the night should precede the evening dusk
Why not lamps right now be appropriated

O "Qateel", we are so attracted to dear earth
Down to earth we come, however over rated

* * *

Tamām Śahr Ke Raste....

tamāma śahra ke raste sajā die jāeṃ
hama ā gae haiṃ to kāṇṭe bichā die jāeṃ

hameṃ sakūna se ika dina qayāma karanā hai
zamīṃ pe dhūpa ke k͟heme lagā die jāeṃ

abhī talaka jo k͟hamośī meṃ ḍālate haiṃ k͟halala
darak͟hta se vo parinde uṛā die jāeṃ

mubādā rāta calī āe śāma se pahale
cirāg͟ha kyoṃ na abhī se bujhā die jāeṃ

"qatīla" apane lie vo kaśiśa zamīna meṃ hai
yahīṃ gireṅge jahāṃ se girā die jāeṃ

* * *

तमाम शह्र के रस्ते.....

तमाम शह्र के रस्ते सजा दिए जाएं
हम आ गए हैं तो कांटे बिछा दिए जाएं

हमें सकून से इक दिन क़याम करना है
ज़मीं पे धूप के खैमे[1] लगा दिए जाएं

अभी तलक जो खमोशी में डालते हैं खलल
दरख्त से वो परिंदे[2] उड़ा दिए जाएं

मुबादा रात चली आए शाम से पहले
चिराग़ क्यों न अभी से बुझा दिए जाएं

"क़तील" अपने लिए वो कशिश[3] ज़मीन में है
यहीं गिरेंगे जहां से गिरा दिए जाएं

* * *

1. तम्बू 2. पक्षी 3. आकर्षण

جو تیرے پیار کا سودا....

جو تیرے پیار کا سودا سروں میں رکھتے ہیں
وہ اپنا کانچ سا دل پتھروں میں رکھتے ہیں

سدا اڑان کی دولت مِلا نہیں کرتی
سنبھال کر اسے پنچھی پروں میں رکھتے ہیں

کسی غریب کا گھر جن سے جگمگا اٹھتا
جلا کے ہم وہ دیئے مقبروں میں رکھتے ہیں

ہُوا ہے جن سے ہمیشہ زیانِ بینائی
ہم اپنی آنکھ انہی منظروں میں رکھتے ہیں

قتیلؔ جتنے بھی ہیں مصلحت کے سوداگر
وہ زندگی کو چھُپا کر گھروں میں رکھتے ہیں

* * *

WHOEVER ARE WITH.....

Whoever are with your love obsessed
Their heart is by an alien power possessed

The ability to sustain flight is not bestowed
Birds keep it well within their feathers pressed

What candles could have lit a poor home homestead
We keep them at mausoleum sites depressed

Whatever is not conducive to our eyes
We are by the same sights focused and impressed

Whoever are merchants of expediency, O "Qateel"
They hide behind the four walls un professed

* * *

Jo Tere Pyār Ke Saudā....

jo tere pyāra kā saudā saroṃ meṃ rakhate haiṃ
vo apanā kām̐ca sā dila pattharoṃ meṃ rakhate haiṃ

sadā uḍāna kī daulata milā nahīṃ karatī
sambhāla kara ise pañchī paroṃ meṃ rakhate haiṃ

kisī g͟harība kā ghara jina se jagamagā uṭhatā
jalā ke hama vo die maqabaroṃ meṃ rakhate haiṃ

huā hai jinase hameśā ziyāna-e-bīnāī
hama apanī āṃkha unhīṃ mañzaroṃ meṃ rakhate haiṃ

"qatīla" jitane bhī haiṃ masalihata ke saudāgara
vo zindagī ko chupā kara gharoṃ meṃ rakhate haiṃ

✸ ✸ ✸

जो तेरे प्यार का सौदा.....

जो तेरे प्यार का सौदा[1] सरों में रखते हैं
वो अपना काँच सा दिल पत्थरों में रखते हैं

सदा उड़ान की दौलत मिला नहीं करती
संभाल कर इसे पंछी परों में रखते हैं

किसी ग़रीब का घर जिन से जगमगा उठता
जला के हम वो दिए मक़बरों में रखते हैं

हुआ है जिनसे हमेशा ज़ियान–ए–बीनाई[2]
हम अपनी आंख उन्हीं मंज़रों[3] में रखते हैं

"क़तील" जितने भी हैं मसलिहत के सौदागर
वो ज़िंदगी को छुपा कर घरों में रखते हैं

* * *

1. जुनून, अन्तिम सीमा को छूती हुई चाहत 2. नज़र का नुक़सान
3. दृश्य

دھوپ ہے، رنگ ہے....

دھوپ ہے، رنگ ہے یا صدا ہے
رات کی بند مٹھی میں کیا ہے

پوچھتا ہے وہ اپنے بدن سے
چاند کھڑکی سے کیوں جھانکتا ہے

دن چڑھے دھوپ میں سونے والا
ہو نہ ہو رات بھر جاگتا ہے

اس قدر خوش ہوں میں اُس سے مل کر
آج رونے کو جی چاہتا ہے

گُنگنایا قتیلؔ اس کو میں نے
اس میں اَب بھی غزل کا مزا ہے

* * *

IS IT SIGHT COLOUR.....

Is it sight colour or sound
In the dead of night, what can be found

Beloved is quizzical about the body
Why moon through the window is profound

Sun up someone asleep in the sun
Must have been insomnolent to confound

I am ecstatic having met beloved today
Tears of joy flow to know no bound

I recited, O "Qateel", some verses
There is in them still some flavour to astound

* * *

Dhūp Hai, Raṅg Hai....

dhūpa hai, raṅga hai yā sadā hai
rāta kī banda muṭṭhī meṃ kyā hai

pūchatā hai vo apane badana se
cāṁda khiḍakī se kyoṃ jhāṅkatā hai

dina caḍhe dhūpa meṃ sone vālā
ho na ho rāta bhara jāgatā hai

isa qadara k͟husa hūṁ maiṃ usase milakara
āja rone ko jī cāhatā hai

guna gunāyā "qatīla" usako mainne
usameṃ aba bhī g͟hazala kā mazā hai

✸ ✸ ✸

धूप है, रंग है.....

धूप है, रंग है या सदा है
रात की बंद मुट्ठी में क्या है

पूछता है वो अपने बदन से
चाँद खिड़की से क्यों झांकता है

दिन चढ़े धूप में सोने वाला
हो न हो रात भर जागता है

इस क़दर खुश हूँ मैं उससे मिलकर
आज रोने को जी चाहता है

गुन गुनाया "क़तील" उसको मैंने
उसमें अब भी ग़ज़ल का मज़ा है

* * *

جیئے گا کون....

جیئے گا کون تمنّا کا باب کھُلنے تک
حروف ہی نہ رہیں گے کتاب کھُلنے تک

ملے گا پھر نہ اُسے کوئی چاہنے والا
یہ سب ہجوم ہے بند نقاب کھُلنے تک

اُمڈ پڑے گا شعاعوں کا سیلِ بے پایاں
وجودِ شب ہے درِ آفتاب کھُلنے تک

یہ کاروبار اجازت بغیر چلتا ہے
لہُو بکے گا، دکانِ شراب کھلنے تک

قتیلؔ عمر کی نقدی سنبھال کر رکھنا
کسی کے نام سے اپنا حساب کھلنے تک

* * *

WHO WILL LIVE.....

Who will live long for a longing to become a fact
Words in the book will vanish before their effect

No one else will pay homage to beloved
The crowd will all melt before any respect

Incessent torrent of sun's rays will be let loose
Tide of night will be swept as a beaten project

This trade will be rampant without any permit
Blood will sell, if not wine, in open contract

Guard your life's savings, O "Qateel", jealously
From your cash lest anyone should to subtract

* * *

Jiegā Kaun....

jiegā kauna tamannā kā bāba khulane taka
harūfa hī na rahenge kitāba khulane taka

milegā phira na use koī cāhane vālā
ye saba hujūma hai banda naqāba khulane taka

umaḍa paḍegā śuāoṃ ko saila-e-bepāyāṃ
vujūda-e-śaba hai dara-e-āfatāba khulane taka

ye kārobāra ijāzata baghaira calatā hai
lahū bikegā, dukāna-e-śarāba khulane taka

"qatila" umra kī naqadī sambhāla kara rakhanā
kisī ke nāma se apanā hisāba khulane taka

* * *

जिएगा कौन.....

जिएगा कौन तमन्ना का बाब[1] खुलने तक
हरूफ़[2] ही न रहेंगे किताब खुलने तक

मिलेगा फिर न उसे कोई चाहने वाला
ये सब हुजूम है बंद नक़ाब खुलने तक

उमड़ पड़ेगा शुआओं[3] को सैल–ए–बेपायां[4]
वुजूद–ए–शब[5] है दर–ए–आफ़ताब[6] खुलने तक

ये कारोबार इजाज़त बग़ैर चलता है
लहू[7] बिकेगा, दुकान–ए–शराब खुलने तक

"क़तील" उम्र की नक़दी संभाल कर रखना
किसी के नाम से अपना हिसाब खुलने तक

* * *

1. द्वार 2. शब्द 3. किरणों 4. असीम तूफ़ान 5. रात का अस्तित्व 6. सूरज का द्वार 7. ख़ून

آ غمِ جاناں....

آ غمِ جاناں بہت دِل گیر ہوں میں
اِک ادھورے خواب کی تعبیر ہوں میں

کل تلک پورے تھے خدو خال میرے
آج بے چہرہ سی اِک تصویر ہوں میں

اَب تو حق موجوں کو ہے مجھ کو مٹا دیں
ریت پر لکھی ہوئی تحریر ہوں میں

ہاتھ میرا تھام لے اے کاش کوئی
راستہ بھُولا ہوا رہ گیر ہوں میں

کس طرح اٹھوں قتیلؔ اس دَر سے آخر
آپ اپنے پاؤں کی زنجیر ہوں میں

* * *

COME O WORLDLY.....

Come O worldly woes, I am in a torment
I am half dreaming, my eyes are dormant

I had, till yesterday, full blown features
Today I am faceless, my picture in a ferment

Woes now have every right to obliterate me
I am a line drawn on sand, to under current subservient

How I wish someone could just hold my hand
I am a way farer, not the way I had meant

How can I, O "Qateel", leave beloved's door
With fetters in my feet, I am quite content

* * *

Ā G͟ham-E-Jānām̐....

ā g͟hama-e-jānām̐ bahuta dila gīra hūm̐ maiṃ
ika adhūre k͟hvāba kī tābīra hūm̐ maiṃ

kala talaka pūre the k͟hada-o-k͟hāla mere
āja be ceharā sī ika tasvīra hūm̐ maiṃ

aba to haqa maujoṃ ko hai mujhako miṭā deṃ
reta para likhī huī taharīra hūm̐ maiṃ

hātha merā thāma le e kāśa koī
rāstā bhūlā huā rahagīra hūm̐ maiṃ

kisa taraha uṭṭhūṃ "qatīla" usa dara se āk͟hira
āpa apane pāṃva kī zañjīra hūm̐ maiṃ

* * *

आ ग़म-ए-जानाँ.....

आ ग़म–ए–जानाँ[1] बहुत दिल गीर[2] हूँ मैं
इक अधूरे ख्वाब की ताबीर हूँ मैं

कल तलक पूरे थे खद–ओ–खाल[3] मेरे
आज बे चेहरा सी इक तस्वीर हूँ मैं

अब तो हक़ मौजों को है मुझको मिटा दें
रेत पर लिखी हुई तहरीर हूँ मैं

हाथ मेरा थाम ले ए काश कोई
रास्ता भूला हुआ रहगीर[4] हूँ मैं

किस तरह उट्ठूं "क़तील" उस दर से आखिर
आप अपने पांव की ज़ंजीर हूँ मैं

* * *

1. महबूबा का ग़म 2. दुःखी मन 3. अंग 4. मुसाफ़िर

بہت دنوں سے....

بہت دنوں سے نہیں اپنے درمیاں وہ شخص
اداس کر کے ہمیں چل دیا کہاں وہ شخص

وہ جس کے نقشِ قدم سے چراغ جلتے تھے
جلے چراغ تو خود بن گیا دھواں وہ شخص

قریب تھا تو کہا ہم نے سنگدل بھی اُسے
ہوا جو دُور تو لگتا ہے جانِ جاں وہ شخص

اس ایک شخص میں تھیں دلربائیاں کیا کیا
ہزار لوگ ملیں گے مگر کہاں وہ شخص

قتیلؔ کیسے بھلائیں ہم اہلِ درد اُسے
دلوں میں چھوڑ گیا اپنی داستاں وہ شخص

* * *

'TIS LONG SINCE.....

'Tis long since that person is not around
Leaving us forlorn, not to be found

One who had lit candles with his candour
Having kindled to become smoke to confound

When so near, we had branded him hard hearted
When afar, that very person seems to surround

That one had embodied thousand attractions
That was one person, though one million abound

How at all we soul mates can forget him, O "Qateel"
In our souls he had left memories so profound

* * *

Bahut Dinoṃ Se....

bahuta dinoṃ se nahīṃ apane daramiyām̐ vo śak̲h̲sa
udāsa karake hameṃ cala diyā kahām̐ vo śak̲h̲sa

vo jisake naqśa-e-qadama se cirāg̲h̲a jalate the
jale cirāg̲h̲a to k̲h̲uda bana gayā dhuām̐ vo śak̲h̲sa

qarība thā to kahā hamane saṅgadila bhī use
huā jo dūra to lagatā hai jāna-e-jām̐ vo śak̲h̲sa

usa eka śak̲h̲sa meṃ thī dila rubāiyām̐ kyā-kyā
hazāra loga mileṅge magara kahām̐ vo śak̲h̲sa

"qatīla" kaise bhulāem̐ hama ahla-e-darda use
diloṃ meṃ chod̂a gayā apanī dāstāṃ vo śak̲h̲sa

✱ ✱ ✱

बहुत दिनों से.....

बहुत दिनों से नहीं अपने दरमियाँ वो शख़्स
उदास करके हमें चल दिया कहाँ वो शख़्स

वो जिसके नक़्श–ए–क़दम[1] से चिराग़ जलते थे
जले चिराग़ तो ख़ुद बन गया धुआँ वो शख़्स

क़रीब था तो कहा हमने संगदिल भी उसे
हुआ जो दूर तो लगता है जान–ए–जाँ वो शख़्स

उस एक शख़्स में थी दिल रुबाइयाँ क्या–क्या
हज़ार लोग मिलेंगे मगर कहाँ वो शख़्स

"क़तील" कैसे भुलाएँ हम अह्ल–ए–दर्द उसे
दिलों में छोड़ गया अपनी दास्तां वो शख़्स

* * *

1. पद–चिन्ह